The SYNAGOGUES *of* EASTERN PENNSYLVANIA

The SYNAGOGUES *of* EASTERN PENNSYLVANIA
A Visual Journey

JULIAN H. PREISLER

AMERICA
THROUGH TIME®
ADDING COLOR TO AMERICAN HISTORY

Front cover top image: Vintage 1910 postcard image of the present Congregation Shaarai Shomayim in Lancaster. Courtesy of the Author's Collection.

Front cover bottom image: Vintage 1950s postcard image of the present Temple Israel in Wilkes-Barre. Courtesy of Special Collections, College of Charleston Libraries.

Back cover image: Vintage image of the 1866 Frank Furness synagogue of Congregation Rodeph Shalom in Philadelphia. Courtesy of Special Collections, College of Charleston Libraries.

America Through Time is an imprint of Fonthill Media LLC
www.through-time.com
office@through-time.com

Published by Arcadia Publishing by arrangement with Fonthill Media LLC
For all general information, please contact Arcadia Publishing:
Telephone: 843-853-2070
Fax: 843-853-0044
E-mail: sales@arcadiapublishing.com
For customer service and orders:
Toll-Free 1-888-313-2665

www.arcadiapublishing.com

First published 2018

Copyright © Julian H. Preisler 2018

ISBN 978-1-63499-064-6

Typeset in Mrs Eaves XL Serif Narrow
Printed in the United States of America

Dedication

Т his book, like many I have done before, is dedicated to the generations before us and those yet to come. Our Jewish history is amazing, and it is always being created, thus we must continue to record and preserve it. I thank my family for always encouraging me to do the work that I love. A special dedication goes to my mother, Dorothy Goldman Preisler (of blessed memory zl'), who passed away in 2015. Her support was constant, and she would be so pleased to know that this particular book came to fruition.

Foreword

Matthew F. Singer, PhD—Philadelphia, Pennsylvania

I t's easy to think we know what's "American" in Jewish-American history. The overwhelming majority of American Jews are educated in public or secular private schools where American history is a firm, substantial, and steady part of the curriculum. If our upbringing includes specifically Jewish education, it typically takes place once, twice or three times a week on Sundays and late-afternoons in synagogue religious or Hebrew school, where limited time and the students' often exhausted attention must focus largely on preparing for bat- or bar-mitzvah. Learning our people's story is part of this mix, but not central. Therefore, when we engage with Jewish-American history as adults, we seek the Jewish element since it's what we don't know. Or so we think.

Julian Preisler's comprehensive and illustrated *Synagogues of Eastern Pennsylvania* reminds us that synagogues are the largest, most enduring, and most public expression of Judaism and Jewishness as conceived and designed by Jews as functional symbols for themselves and representations in the built landscape for all to see and consider. But we tend to look at them in isolation or, at most, as part of a given community. The truth is that clear trends in synagogue architecture give lasting, physical shape to what are often abstract and conceptual changes in American culture and Jewish-Americans' perceptions of their place in America. If we know what we're looking for, we can see in every synagogue a piece of a national story.

Within American history, Pennsylvania's story is distinct, marked by the establishment of key and abiding precedents that shaped the entire country. It is singular even in the company of the twelve other colonies that fought to become states and establish a nation. Pennsylvania and Rhode Island were the first colonies founded (in 1663 and 1681, respectively) with explicit commitments to freedom of religion, and by extension and as practiced, the concepts of separation of church and state and multiculturalism. William Penn's Holy Experiment—the establishment, promotion, nurture, and enlightened governance of the colony of Pennsylvania—surpassed Rhode Island's example by being a concerted and comprehensive act of faith and vision for governance. It was inspired by and built upon Penn's (1644-1718) Quaker beliefs and the persecution that he and other Quakers suffered as resolute dissenters from the Church of England. The charter for Pennsylvania that Penn drafted in 1682 stated his hopes for a political, material, and spiritual utopia.

Penn actively encouraged immigration from non-British countries. He distributed a prospectus throughout Europe that emphasized the political and religious freedom of Pennsylvania as well as the colony's bountiful natural resources, its rich farmland prime among them. Groups persecuted in Europe and less tolerant American colonies—Jewish, Amish, Mennonite, Huguenot,

Catholic, and others—found sanctuary in Philadelphia and other parts of Pennsylvania. Penn held Jews in special regard since, as indicated in the book *The Select Works of William Penn*, Jews "had a measure of light, some divine seed sown in their heart, some talents given."[1]

Philadelphia was one of only five American cities with Jewish communities large enough to sustain Jewish congregations as of 1776; it was joined by fellow Atlantic coastal port cities Charleston, Newport, New York, and Savannah. Perhaps tellingly, a possible sixth was inland in Pennsylvania—Lancaster—but the community was small and virtually disappeared between 1804 and 1856. The diversity promoted by Penn can be seen in the relatively peaceful pluralism within Philadelphia's Jewish community. Philadelphia was the first city in the US to have two Jewish congregations, one Sephardi and one Ashkenazi: Mikveh Israel (founded c. 1740) and Rodeph Shalom (founded c. 1795), respectively.

What makes this book so significant beyond its stated geographical range—eastern Pennsylvania—is that the story of Jewish life and synagogues in the region is not limited to, and often not at all influenced by, the major general and Jewish population center of Philadelphia. Stable but small Jewish communities emerged in the modest cities and towns of Allentown, Pottsville, Reading, Scranton and Wilkes-Barre by the 1830s and 1840s. While not far from the Atlantic, these were definitively inland settlements surrounded by miles of farmland. They were places where the Jewish peddler-cum-retailer became a necessary part of the economy, was recognized and respected for civic contribution, and built a personal, professional, familial and communal legacy. This model for Jewish entry into American society became the prevailing one throughout the nineteenth century into the early twentieth in every region of the country.

In this and many other ways, Julian Preisler's *Synagogues of Eastern Pennsylvania* shows and tells a story not limited to the region specified in its title, but one that resonates with all of Jewish-American history and its quintessential monument: the synagogue. Here you'll find numerous synagogues of various vintages, sizes and shapes in a single metropolitan area; sprinkled throughout suburbs; and standing alone—some having lost their congregations—in smaller towns in areas that are still rural or became coalfields or sites for steel manufacturing and other industries. In large American cities, such as Philadelphia, there are many ways to be and do Jewish without joining a synagogue. In small-town America, the synagogue is the center of Jewish life, and membership and participation in its activities is the way to express one's Jewishness. Eastern Pennsylvania is within the Great Northeastern Megalopolis, but that powerfully urban association belies the varieties of deeply ingrained ways of life within the region. Expanding the words of Walt Whitman's poem *Song of Myself* outward from the individual, it "contains multitudes." It is America.

Acknowledgments

A book like this takes enormous time and effort to bring together and would not be possible without the interest and enthusiasm of many people and institutions. I would like to thank all the congregations and their staff and members who provided me with information and photographs. A special thank you is extended to the following people and institutions especially cooperative in bringing this project to fruition: David Brenner (Shaarai Shomayim, Lancaster); Daniel Bubnis; Joe and Judith Clark (Beth Israel, Lebanon); Rabbi Jon Cutler (Beth Israel, Eagle); Art Glantz (Temple Israel, Stroudsburg); Karen Ernest and Amy Wissoker Graham (Ohev Shalom Congregation, Wallingford); Ruth Ellen Gruber; Elliott Kleinman (Beth Israel, Honesdale); Valerie Landis (B'nai Jacob, Phoenixville); Jane Messinger (Temple Israel, Wilkes-Barre); Alyssa Neely and Dale Rosengarten (College of Charleston [SC] Library); Phil Nordlinger (Shir Ami, Newtown); Ohav Zedek (Wilkes-Barre); Michelle Rohrbach (Beth El, Allentown); Karen Samuels; Samantha Seidel (Easton); Matthew Singer, (Philadelphia); Judy Trias (Beth Or, Maple Glen); Steven Vale (Temple Israel, Scranton); Micki Wechsler (Brith Sholom, Bethlehem). A huge thank you goes to Richard W. Clark for everything especially his long hours of proofreading and editing.

Contents

Dedication   5

Foreword   7

Acknowledgments   9

Introduction   13

1   The Southeast Region   15

2   The Lehigh Valley and Lebanon Valley Regions   80

3   The Pocono Mountain Region   101

4   The Anthracite Coal Mining Region   108

Introduction

I love synagogue architecture and history. For those of you who may have read my other books, that fact is clearly evident. It makes no difference whether they are modest or grand, small or large or urban, suburban or small town. They all have a story to tell. My goal with *The Synagogues of Eastern Pennsylvania* is to provide an informal look at the synagogues and Jewish history in the Eastern portion of the Keystone State. It is a companion volume to *The Synagogues of Central and Western Pennsylvania*, from 2014. This book is not meant to be an in-depth or scholarly work, but one that appeals to a wide-ranging audience and provides the reader with a visual journey through history and style. My primary focus is on the synagogues that are still active, though I always try to include as much information and vintage images as possible of synagogues that no longer exist. Photograph and text limits are always an unfortunate, but necessary consideration. Philadelphia alone has such a huge number of synagogues—current, former and demolished—that it was impossible to include them all. In the other regions of Eastern Pennsylvania, I tried to include all of the extant synagogues as much as possible, with a selection of either images or history of those synagogues that have been closed or demolished.

With the sixth largest Jewish population in the United States, Pennsylvania has hundreds of synagogues and they come in all shapes, sizes and styles. Pennsylvania is unique with regard to the extensive number of locations that either have, or once had, functioning Jewish congregations and communities. While the city of Philadelphia, no doubt, has a large number of synagogues, both current and former, synagogues were established in many of the towns found along the industrial and mining routes of Eastern Pennsylvania. By presenting images of these many synagogues, especially the ones that are no longer used for Jewish worship, not only is their history documented, but the uniqueness and wealth of architecture is shared for all. This diversity of architecture reflects that very same diversity of the Jewish communities that settled throughout the Commonwealth.

Jewish life thrives in Philadelphia and its suburbs, but it also is strong in the smaller cities such as Allentown, Bethlehem, Easton, Scranton and Wilkes-Barre. Because the region is no longer the manufacturing and industrial giant it once was, the Jewish population has seen a decline, but dedicated Jewish congregations continue the tradition of Jewish worship, philanthropy, education and community. There are many locations that no longer have Jewish populations or functioning synagogues. Luckily, many of the former synagogues still stand.

This book is part history, travel guide and photograph collection. The photographs and information contained in this book help to tell the diverse story of Jewish congregational life and its architectural history in Eastern Pennsylvania. Visuals provide a moment-in-time feeling as you flip through the pages of the book. So why is a book like this important? My interest in history and synagogue architecture goes back nearly forty years. This is my passion, and it is vital that we document our built Jewish environment and share what we find. Change is natural part of the life of any community; documenting and recording the past for future generations ensures that the changes we experience do not negate so much of what came before. Placing importance on our past is as vital as the time and energy given to the present and future of our communities.

1

The Southeast Region

The Southeast region of Pennsylvania, including Philadelphia, is home to the largest Jewish population in the state. Philadelphia has the distinction of being the fourth oldest Jewish Community in the United States, having been established in 1740 with the founding of the Mikveh Israel Cemetery and shortly thereafter the Mikveh Israel Congregation. The area includes Philadelphia City as well as Bucks, Chester, Delaware and Montgomery Counties, along with Lancaster County, the heart of the famous Pennsylvania Dutch Country.

Bucks County

Bucks County, adjacent to Philadelphia and Montgomery Counties, is home today to a growing Jewish community. Much of the growth has occurred in recent years, as population shifted from the Jewish areas of Northeast Philadelphia to adjacent Bucks County. However, there was a Jewish presence in the county as early 1896. That year, Philadelphia Rabbi Joseph Krauskopf purchased a 100-acre farm in Doylestown, arranged for the construction of a classroom, hired two faculty members, and began the National Farm School. Rabbi Krauskopf had traveled to Russia two years earlier to appeal in person to the Czar to allow his Jewish subjects to own and farm land. When the appeal was turned down, Krauskopf returned to America with the idea of a school that would give young Jewish men from the congested cities the opportunity to gain agricultural experience along with academics. Though his efforts concentrated on bringing Jews back to the land, the school welcomed men of all faiths. From this humble start began what is now the Delaware Valley University.

Ahavath Achim Congregation, established in 1904 in Bristol Borough, was the first Jewish congregation in the county. The congregation later became the Bristol Jewish Center and built a synagogue at 216 Pond Street in 1948. Due to population shifts and a dwindling membership, the synagogue closed in 2015 and merged with Congregation Kol Emet, a Reconstructionist congregation in Yardley in Lower Makefield Township. The old synagogue is now used by the county.

Tiferes Israel Congregation in Warrington is now the oldest Jewish congregation in the county, opened in 1923 and chartered in 1924. Harry Cohn initiated it in 1910 when he brought his family to the area along with a Torah that he brought from Russia. When Harry Cohn died in 1943, Jewish families had largely disappeared from the area, though his sons kept up the original 1924 synagogue and the small congregation held regular services. In 1957, the Philadelphia Jewish

Exponent ran an article called "Synagogue in Search of a Congregation," sparking a rebirth and subsequent growth of the congregation. The independent congregation is now located at 2478 Street Road in Warrington. The sanctuary was built circa 1962 and major renovations began on the synagogue in 2006. It was rededicated in 2012. It houses the ark, lecterns and memorial plaques from the former Adath Shalom synagogue in South Philadelphia, which closed in 2007.

During the 1950s new Jewish congregations were established in Bucks County as Levittown and other areas were developed. Temple Shalom was established around 1951 in Levittown and closed in 2011, when it merged with Shir Ami Congregation in Newtown. The former Temple Shalom on Edgely Road is now a regional office for Easter Seals. Congregation Beth El was established in 1953 in the Levittown area. In the 1990s the congregation relocated to Yardley and in 2008 dedicated a new synagogue on Stony Hill Road. Beth Chaim in Feasterville was founded in 1956 and built their synagogue on East Street Road beginning in 1957. In 2006, the congregation merged with Shaare Shomayim in Northeast Philadelphia. Temple Judea was established in 1959 in Doylestown and built their first synagogue in 1967. In 2013 a new temple was dedicated in nearby Furlong. Congregation Shir Ami began as the Buck County Jewish Congregation in 1976. Ohev Shalom Congregation also began in 1976 in Richboro. Adath Tikvah-Montefiore Congregation in Northeast Philadelphia merged with Ohev Shalom in 2003, and the campus is named in honor of the former congregation. Their former synagogue, built in 1953 at Summerdale and Hoffnagle streets in Northeast Philadelphia, was home to Stern Hebrew High School until 2010. The Reconstructionist Congregation Kol Emet was established in 1984 and is located in Yardley.

Other synagogues in Bucks County include Congregation Brothers of Israel, which was established in 1883 in nearby Trenton, New Jersey. This Conservative congregation relocated to Bucks County in 2007 and purchased a large church, which they converted for use as their synagogue. Brothers of Israel was the last Jewish congregation to leave Trenton. The Reconstructionist congregation Kehilat HaNahar began in 1994. Their synagogue on West Mechanic Street in New Hope is known as the "Little Shul by the River." Tzedek v Shalom, another Bucks County Reconstructionist congregation, is located in Newtown. In addition, Chabad Lubavitch has several locations in the county, including the one that was the former Temple Judea on Swamp Road and The Shul at Yardley. Kehilas B'nai Shalom is an Orthodox congregation that is part of the Bensalem Jewish Outreach Center.

Bensalem (Bucks County): Congregation Tifereth Israel; Exterior of the current Bristol Road synagogue, 2007. [Courtesy of Jeffrey J. Barnett.]

Bristol (Bucks County): Bristol Jewish Center-Ahavath Achim; Exterior of the former Pond Street synagogue, 2007. [Courtesy of Alan J. Vogenberg.]

Doylestown (Bucks County): Temple Judea; Exterior of the former East Swamp Road temple, 1991. [Courtesy of the Author's Collection.]

Furlong (Bucks County): Temple Judea; Exterior view of the present Rogers Road temple in Doylestown Township. [Courtesy of Temple Judea.]

Levittown (Bucks County): Congregation Beth El; Exterior of the former Penn Valley Road synagogue (demolished), 1991. [Courtesy of the Author's Collection.] See also: Yardley.

Levittown (Bucks County): Temple Shalom; Exterior of the former Edgely Road temple, 1990. [Courtesy of the Author's Collection.]

Above left: **Levittown (Bucks County):** Temple Shalom; Sanctuary interior of the former Edgely Road temple, n.d. [Courtesy of Shir Ami Congregation, Newtown.]

Above right: **Newtown (Bucks County):** Shir Ami Congregation; Exterior of the present Richboro Road synagogue, 1990. [Courtesy of the Author's Collection.]

Newtown (Bucks County): Shir Ami Congregation; Exterior of the present Richboro Road synagogue, 2017. [Courtesy of Shir Ami Congregation.]

Newtown (Bucks County): Shir Ami Congregation; Sanctuary interior of the Richboro Road synagogue, 2017. [Courtesy of Shir Ami Congregation.]

Above left: **Richboro (Bucks County):** Ohev Shalom of Bucks County; Exterior of the present Second Street Pike synagogue, 1990. [Courtesy of the Author's Collection.]

Above right: **Warrington (Bucks County):** Congregation Tiferes B'nai Israel; Exterior of the present Street Road synagogue, 2008. [Courtesy of the Author's Collection.]

Above: **Yardley (Bucks County):** Congregation Kol Emet; Exterior of the present Oxford Valley Road synagogue, 2017. [Courtesy of Congregation Kol Emet.]

Below: **Yardley (Bucks County):** Congregation Kol Emet; Sanctuary interior of the present Oxford Valley Road synagogue, 2017. [Courtesy of Congregation Kol Emet.]

Chester County

Chester County has also experienced an increase it its Jewish population in recent years. Like Bucks County, it also had early Jewish roots. The three earliest Jewish congregations in Chester County are Beth Israel in Eagle, B'nai Jacob in Phoenixville, and Kesher Israel in West Chester. Congregation Beth Israel was formed in 1904 in Coatesville as Congregation Kesher Israel and was chartered as Beth Israel in 1916. Their Coatesville synagogue was built in 1924 and was in use until 1995, when the congregation moved to Eagle in Upper Uwchland Twp. The former synagogue still stands and is now a church. In 1979, Beth Israel was the first Conservative congregation to hire a woman rabbi, who was also the first openly gay Conservative rabbi. Congregation B'nai Jacob in Phoenixville was organized in 1912. They built their synagogue at Starr and Manavon streets in 1957 and expanded the facility in the 1990s. Kesher Israel Congregation was established in 1914. Their synagogue in West Chester Borough, built in 1924, was designed by the noted Philadelphia architect Norman N. Rice. That synagogue still stands on North Church Street. In 1988, Kesher Israel built a new synagogue on Pottstown Pike in West Chester Township. The synagogue was designed to evoke the historic wooden synagogues that were once a fixture in Eastern Europe.

Newer Jewish congregations in Chester County include Or Shalom in Berwyn, established in 1974 and located on Darby-Paoli Road. The oldest portion of the synagogue was originally a church built in 1962. Or Shalom was the first synagogue on the far western edge of the "Main Line," an informally delineated historical and social region of suburban Philadelphia, lying along the former Pennsylvania Railroad's once prestigious Main Line. In Malvern, also along the Main Line there is Beth Chaim Reform Congregation, established in 1992. Their synagogue on Conestoga Road was built in 2007. Other synagogues in Chester County include The Chabad Center in Devon and Makon Kadosh: The Jewish Fellowship of Chester County located in West Chester.

Berwyn (Chester County): Congregation Or Shalom; Exterior of the present Darby-Paoli Road synagogue, 2008. [Courtesy of Julie Miller and Congregation Or Shalom.]

Coatesville (Chester County): Congregation Beth Israel; Vintage postcard of the former Fifth and Harmony Streets synagogue, n.d. [Courtesy of Special Collections, College of Charleston Libraries.]

Eagle (Chester County): Congregation Beth Israel; Exterior of the present Pottstown Pike synagogue, 2017. [Courtesy of Rabbi Jon Cutler and Congregation Beth Israel.]

Eagle (Chester County): Congregation Beth Israel; Sanctuary and Ark view of the present Pottstown Pike synagogue, 2017. [Courtesy of Rabbi Jon Cutler and Congregation Beth Israel.]

Malvern (Chester County): Beth Chaim Reform Congregation; Exterior of the present Conestoga Road synagogue, 2007. [Courtesy of Len Shyles and Beth Chaim Reform Congregation.]

Phoenixville (Chester County): Congregation B'nai Jacob; Exterior of the present Manavon Street synagogue and center, 2017. [Courtesy of Congregation B'nai Jacob.]

Above left: **Phoenixville (Chester County):** Congregation B'nai Jacob; Sanctuary interior of the present Manavon Street synagogue and center, 2017. [Courtesy of Congregation B'nai Jacob.]

Above right: **West Chester (Chester County):** Kesher Israel Congregation; Exterior of the former Church street synagogue, 1993. [Courtesy of the Author's Collection.]

West Chester (Chester County): Kesher Israel Congregation; Exterior of the present Pottstown Pike synagogue, 1994. [Courtesy of the Author's Collection.]

West Chester (Chester County): Kesher Israel Congregation; Interior of the present Pottstown Pike synagogue, n.d. [Courtesy of Clear Sound Media, Inc., Yeadon, Pennsylvania.]

Delaware County

Delaware County, adjacent to Chester, Montgomery and Philadelphia counties, has the earliest Jewish Community established outside of the City of Philadelphia proper. Hendrick Jacobs and Ephriam Herman, two Jewish peddlers, were the first recorded Jews in Delaware County, being listed as taxable persons in Upland. It was not until after the Civil War that Jews settled permanently in Delaware County in the city of Chester. The Brandeis and Turk families were of German origin and arrived prior to 1859 and the 1880s respectively. Both families were engaged in the retail clothing trades. The Jewish presence in Chester increased as a number of Jewish families came to the area from Philadelphia and as immigrant Jewish families settled in Chester.

The dream of a formal Jewish organization came to fruition in 1891 when B'nai Israel was formally organized as an Orthodox Jewish congregation. It was chartered in 1903 as the Congregation of Israel. They dedicated a synagogue in 1904 at Third and Lloyd streets in Chester. Land for a Jewish cemetery (Brookhaven Cemetery in nearby Brookhaven Borough) was procured in 1910 by the local Ahavas Israel Lodge. In 1915 B'nai Aaron Congregation was chartered. About the same time Congregation Mispallelim was formed by a splinter group of members from both B'nai Israel and B'nai Aaron. Their synagogue was built in 1949 at 325 West Seventh Street and still stands. In 1925-26, the Directors of the Young Men's Hebrew Association purchased land on Eighth Street near Welsh for a synagogue-center which they deeded to the Ohev Shalom Congregation, which had formed in 1920 by the merger of B'nai Israel and B'nai Aaron. The new Ohev Shalom Synagogue Center was dedicated in 1927. In the 1930s, Ohev Shalom officially joined the United Synagogue of America, the Conservative wing of American Jews. Congregation Mishpalellim held groundbreaking ceremonies for their synagogue in October 1949.

By 1957, the Ohev Shalom Synagogue Center was becoming crowded and outdated, and fundraising began for purchasing land at Providence and Chester roads in Nether Providence Township. Percival Goodman was chosen as architect; over the decades, he designed over 50 synagogues. The new facility was dedicated in March 1965. As more families began moving to the suburban areas around Chester City, Congregation Mispallelim merged with Ohev Shalom in 1973, thus ending the Jewish physical presence in Chester City.

By 1925, the Borough of Media had enough Jewish families to form Congregation Beth Israel, led by Harry Dramann and Isadore Kashinsky. The congregation held its first High Holy Day services the following year, and in 1929 Beth Israel was granted a charter. After many years of holding services in rented quarters, the congregation dedicated a permanent synagogue in 1938 on Gayley Street in central Media. The two-story building had previously housed a Quaker school. After many years of growth and then decline in the 1960s, the congregation made a bold move in 1970 to affiliate with the Reconstructionist Rabbinical College and affiliated fully in 1972 with what many call the "Fourth Movement of American Judaism." It is the oldest Reconstructionist congregation in the Philadelphia region. Continued steady growth and the need for additional and accessible space resulted in the move to the current synagogue on South New Middletown Road in 1997.

Darby Borough, Yeadon Borough, and Upper Darby Township saw the formation of Jewish congregations as early as the 1920s, as the Jewish population began spilling over from various West and South Philadelphia neighborhoods. Congregation Agudath Achim of Darby and Collingdale was formed in the 1920s. In 1963, it merged with what was to become the Suburban Jewish Community Center-B'nai Aaron in Havertown. Temple Israel, a Conservative congregation in

Upper Darby, was established around 1945. Their Colonial Revival style synagogue on Walnut Street and Bywood Avenue was built in 1950. As the Jewish presence in the area declined toward the end of the twentieth century, Temple Israel merged with Congregation Beth El Ner Tamid in nearby Broomall in 2002. The site is now the Municipal Branch library dedicated in 2011. The Upper Darby Synagogue-Center also existed in the 1950s. In Yeadon Borough, the Yeadon Jewish Community Center-Beth Tefilah was established in 1945. The Conservative congregation dedicated their new synagogue at Whitby Avenue and West Cobbs Creek Parkway in 1949, and a school wing was added in 1953. By 1991, there were not enough Jewish residents in the area to sustain a congregation, and they merged with the Suburban Jewish Community Center-B'nai Aaron in Havertown. The old synagogue is now a church.

Havertown's Suburban Jewish Community Center-B'nai Aaron was formed in 1969 by the merger of B'nai Aaron of the Wynnfield section of Philadelphia, established in 1926, and the Suburban Jewish Community Center Tel Or of Delaware County, established in 1951. Due to the decline in Jewish residents in the area, the congregation closed in 2011 and merged with Adath Israel Congregation in Merion Station. Their former synagogue on Mill Road in Havertown was built in stages between 1954 and 1973. It is now a church. Springfield, at one time, also had a synagogue, Congregation Ner Tamid-Delaware County Jewish Community Center. The congregation was established in 1957, and their school-like synagogue was constructed in 1960. In 1992, the congregation closed and merged with Broomall's Beth El Suburban, forming Congregation Beth El-Ner Tamid. The former Springfield synagogue still stands.

Broomall is home to two Jewish congregations, Temple Sholom and Congregation Beth El Ner Tamid. Temple Shalom was established in the 1950s as the Broomall Reform Temple. Their synagogue is located on North Church Lane. Congregation Beth El Ner Tamid was begun in 1956 as Beth El Suburban and was sponsored by Congregation Beth El of West Philadelphia, established in 1904. Their synagogue is located on Paxon Hollow Road and was built in stages beginning in 1964. In 1972, Tikvas Israel of West Philadelphia, which was founded in 1920, merged with the congregation. Though Delaware County has experienced synagogue closings and mergers, the four synagogues in the county today plus a Chabad Center are strong stable congregations serving the Jewish population of the county.

Broomall (Delaware County): Congregation Beth El Ner Tamid; Exterior of the present Paxon Hollow Road synagogue, 2008. [Courtesy of Arthur Rosenthal.]

Broomall (Delaware County): Temple Sholom; Exterior of the present Church Road temple, 1990. [Courtesy of the Author's Collection.]

Chester (Delaware County): Congregation Mispallelim; Exterior of the former Seventh Street synagogue, 1973. [Courtesy of Congregation Ohev Shalom.]

Chester (Delaware County): Congregation Mispallelim; Interior of the former Seventh Street synagogue, 1973. [Courtesy of Congregation Ohev Shalom.]

Above left: **Chester (Delaware County):** Ohev Sholom Synagogue Center; Exterior of the former East Eighth and Welsh Streets synagogue center, n.d. [Courtesy of Congregation Ohev Shalom.] See also: Wallingford.

Above right: **Chester (Delaware County):** Ohev Sholom Synagogue Center; Sanctuary interior of the former East Eighth and Welsh Streets synagogue center. [Courtesy of Congregation Ohev Shalom.]

Havertown (Delaware County): Suburban Jewish Community Center-B'nai Aaron; Exterior of the former Mill Road synagogue, 1994. [Photograph by Julian H. Preisler.]

Media (Delaware County): Congregation Beth Israel; Exterior of the present South New Middletown Road synagogue, 2018. [Courtesy of Congregation Beth Israel and John Greenstine.]

Media (Delaware County): Congregation Beth Israel; Sanctuary interior of the present South New Middletown Road synagogue, 2018. [Courtesy of Congregation Beth Israel and John Greenstine.]

Media (Delaware County): Congregation Beth Israel; Exterior of the former Gayley Street synagogue, 1993. [Courtesy of the Author's Collection.]

Upper Darby (Delaware County: Temple Israel; Facade and entrance of the former Walnut Street and Bywood Avenue synagogue, 1992. [Courtesy of the Author's Collection.]

Upper Darby (Delaware County: Temple Israel; Exterior of the former Walnut Street and Bywood Avenue synagogue, 1992. [Courtesy of the Author's Collection.]

Wallingford (Delaware County: Congregation Ohev Shalom; Exterior of the newly completed Chester Road synagogue, circa 1964. [Courtesy of Congregation Ohev Shalom.]

Wallingford (Delaware County: Congregation Ohev Shalom; Front facade of the present Chester Road synagogue, 2017. [Courtesy of Congregation Ohev Shalom.]

Wallingford (Delaware County: Congregation Ohev Shalom; Sanctuary interior of the present Chester Road synagogue, 2017. [Courtesy of Congregation Ohev Shalom.]

Yeadon (Delaware County): Yeadon Jewish Community Center-Beth Tefilah; Exterior view of the former West Cobbs Creek Parkway and Whitby Avenue synagogue, 1990. [Courtesy of the Author's Collection.]

Yeadon (Delaware County): Yeadon Jewish Community Center-Beth Tefilah; Entrance of the former West Cobbs Creek Parkway and Whitby Avenue synagogue, 1990. [Courtesy of the Author's Collection.]

Lancaster County

The City of Lancaster has two distinct periods of Jewish history and was the second place that Jews settled in Pennsylvania after Philadelphia. The first practicing Jew to make Lancaster his permanent home was Joseph Simon who arrived around 1740. Other Jews came to Lancaster between 1740 and 1790 and formed the core of a small first Jewish community. Lancaster's colonial Jewish population was fluid and quite mobile. They were traders with Native Americans, merchants, landowners and tradesmen and many had family and business connections to Philadelphia, New York and other colonial cities.

In 1747 Joseph Simon and Isaac Nunes Henriques purchased a half-acre of land in Lancaster for a cemetery in trust for the Society of Jews. It is the fourth oldest Jewish burial ground in the US. Formal Jewish congregations were slow to form in Colonial America, but Jewish worship and ritual practices were observed in Lancaster by the early Jewish families. A room in Joseph Simon's home served as the place of worship. A portion of the wooden ark used in Simon's home is now part of the collection of the Museum of American Jewish History in Philadelphia. One of Simon's Torahs used is on display as well on loan from Philadelphia's Mikveh Israel Congregation. Joseph Simon died in 1804 and he was the last colonial Jew to reside in Lancaster.

Starting in the mid 1840s Jews of German descent would settle in Lancaster. In 1856 Congregation Shaarai Shomayim was chartered by twenty-one Jewish men forming the basis of an enduring Jewish community. In 1867 the congregation dedicated its first permanent home, a small but elegant brick synagogue on the southwest corner of East Orange and North Christian streets. The synagogue was extensively renovated in 1888. The congregation remained there until 1896 when the present Renaissance Revival style synagogue at Duke and James streets was built. As Rabbi Isaac Mayer Wise, the "father" of Reform Judaism in America, arrived to dedicate the synagogue, a gas explosion resulted in injury and damage. The temple was repaired, and a second dedication took place. Shaarai Shomayim began as an Orthodox congregation with German the language of services, the school and congregational records. In 1888 the congregation officially became Reform. The historic temple has been expanded and renovated several times over the years. A school addition was built in 1960. An expansion project completed in 2000 refashioned the building elements into a cohesive unit. The Colonial era Jewish cemetery has been enlarged and improved by the congregation.

Eastern European and Russian Orthodox Jews came to Lancaster starting in the 1880s. The first Orthodox congregation, Chizuk Emunah, was chartered in 1887. Hagudah Sholom, a second Orthodox congregation, was chartered in 1892. A third, Degel Israel, was chartered in 1896 and a fourth congregation, Kesher Torah, was chartered in 1911. Degel Israel built the first Orthodox synagogue in Lancaster at 416 Chester Street in 1900. The other Orthodox congregations were splinter groups and by 1920 they had all come together under the banner of Congregation Degel Israel. The Chester Street synagogue featured windows given to them by Shaarai Shomayim from their old Orange Street Temple.

The synagogue was enlarged in 1911 but was heavily damaged in a fire in 1923. The synagogue was rebuilt and expanded once again in 1929 and in use along with auxiliary buildings until 1964 when the present mid-century modern synagogue was dedicated at 1120 Columbia Pike in Lancaster Township.

The youngest Jewish congregation in Lancaster is Temple Beth El chartered in 1945 by members of the Jewish community who desired the Conservative form of worship and ritual which is positioned between the Orthodox and Reform. The former Baker Mansion at 25 North Lime Street was purchased in 1945 for use as the synagogue. An educational wing and social hall were added in 1962 and enlarged in 1965. The congregation remained downtown until 2002 when a large new synagogue was built at 1836 Rohrerstown Road in East Hempfield Township.

It is interesting to note that in the city of Ephrata, twelve miles from Lancaster there existed a Jewish civic, philanthropic and social group formed in 1936 as The Ephrata Hebrew Circle. In 1958 a building on South State Street was purchased to house the group's activities. The population of Jews in Ephrata decreased and by the 1970s the building had been sold.

Above: **Lancaster (Lancaster County):** Temple Beth El; Exterior of the present Rohrerstown Pike synagogue, 2008. [Courtesy of the Author's Collection.]

Below: **Lancaster (Lancaster County):** Temple Beth El; Exterior of the Lime Street synagogue, 1989. [Courtesy of the Author's Collection.]

Above left: **Lancaster (Lancaster County):** Temple Beth El; Exterior of the Lime Street synagogue and addition, 1989. [Courtesy of the Author's Collection.]

Above right: **Lancaster (Lancaster County):** Degel Israel Congregation; Exterior of the Chester Street synagogue, n.d. [Courtesy of David Brenner.]

Lancaster (Lancaster County): Degel Israel Congregation; Sanctuary interior of the Chester Street synagogue, n.d. [Courtesy of David Brenner.]

Lancaster (Lancaster County): Degel Israel Congregation; Exterior of the present Columbia Pike synagogue, n.d. [Courtesy of the Author's Collection.]

Lancaster (Lancaster County): Congregation Shaarai Shomayim; Exterior of the old Orange Street Temple, circa 1875. [Courtesy of David Brenner and Congregation Shaarai Shomayim.]

Above left: **Lancaster (Lancaster County):** Congregation Shaarai Shomayim; Sanctuary interior of the old Orange Street Temple with Rabbi Ungerleider, 1888. [Courtesy of David Brenner and Congregation Shaarai Shomayim.]

Above right: **Lancaster (Lancaster County):** Congregation Shaarai Shomayim; Exterior of the present Duke Street Temple, 1897. [Courtesy of David Brenner and Congregation Shaarai Shomayim.]

Lancaster (Lancaster County): Congregation Shaarai Shomayim; Sanctuary interior of the Duke Street Temple pre air-conditioning, circa 1956. [Courtesy of David Brenner and Congregation Shaarai Shomayim.]

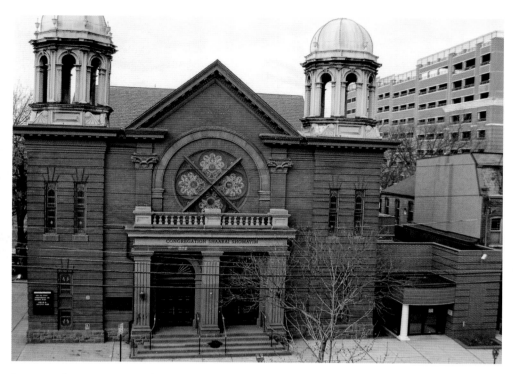

Lancaster (Lancaster County): Congregation Shaarai Shomayim; Front facade of the present Duke Street Temple, 2018. [Courtesy of David Brenner and Congregation Shaarai Shomayim.]

Lancaster (Lancaster County): Congregation Shaarai Shomayim; Side view of the Duke Street Temple exterior and addition, 2018. [Courtesy of David Brenner and Congregation Shaarai Shomayim.]

Montgomery County

Montgomery County is primarily a suburban county northwest of Philadelphia but contains both farm land as well as densely populated areas close to Philadelphia. The Jewish community in Montgomery County is one of the largest in the region, with many Jewish congregations originally established in Philadelphia, newer congregations, and large synagogues.

The oldest Jewish community still in existence in the county is found in Pottsville. German Jewish families began settling in Pottstown in the 1840s in the area called Chicken Hill. By 1859, the Miller, Mosheim and Weitzenkorn families also settled in Pottstown. Other Jewish families arrived from Hungary and Russia, settling in the Pottstown area between 1882 and 1890. Services were held in homes until 1889 when a charter was granted to create Congregation Ahavas Achim and a new synagogue was built on Hale Street. Unfortunately, financial and other problems forced the congregation to dissolve and sell the Hale Street property. The cemetery they established still exists. In 1892, the Hesed Shel Emet Congregation was established and granted a charter. They purchased the Hale Street property the following year. In 1925, the congregation dedicated a new synagogue at High and Warren streets. It was a large, elegant synagogue with Italianate style towers, stained glass windows and a Star of David carved into the top of the facade. Growth necessitated a larger space and around 1962 a new, modern, tent-like synagogue was built at 575 North Keim Street. The facade features Judaica metal sculptures and stained-glass windows. As the Conservative congregation became smaller over the years they entered a partnership with the Bethel Community Church and the building was sold to them in 2016 after having leased space there since 2015. Both congregations will use the building and Hesed Shel Emet will continue to serve the local Jewish Community.

Norristown, the county seat, was once an industrial, manufacturing, banking and retail hub. The Jewish community was established in 1892, when the German Hebrew Society of Norristown was chartered. In 1901, a new charter formed Congregation Tiferes Israel. A local Young Men's Hebrew Association was also formed. The synagogue's first synagogue, a former church, was at the corner of Marshall and Cherry streets. A later location was on Swede Street. In 1936, the Jewish Community Center (former YMHA) merged with Tiferes Israel Congregation, located at Powell and Brown streets. A new auditorium was built in 1948, a new sanctuary in 1957, and another addition in 1969. In 1989 Congregation Beth Israel of Lansdale merged with the Norristown Jewish Center Tiferes Israel to become Tiferet Bet Israel, and the congregation built a new synagogue on Skippack Pike in Blue Bell. Stained-glass windows, memorial plaques and a Tree of Life were moved from the previous buildings to the new synagogue. The old synagogue-center in Norristown still stands. The old Beth Israel on Sumneytown Pike in Lansdale is now a church.

Elkins Park begins at the northern city line of Philadelphia. The inner-ring suburb has the largest concentration of Jewish congregations in Montgomery County and also some of the biggest. Most of the congregations relocated from North Philadelphia as the Jewish population moved into the suburbs in the 1950s. Congregation Beth Sholom in Elkins Park has the distinction of being the only synagogue ever designed by the architect Frank Lloyd Wright. Originally located in the Logan section of Philadelphia, the congregation was established in 1917 as the Logan Congregation Ahavas Israel. It was chartered in 1919 as Beth Sholom. Their North Broad and Courtland streets synagogue was built in 1922 and still stands. In the 1940s a school and center were established in Elkins Park and the congregation relocated completely to Elkins Park, when their monumental Old York Road synagogue was completed in 1959. It is listed on the National Register of Historic Places.

Adath Jeshurun, also on Old York Road, was established in 1858 in Philadelphia. Their first synagogue was built in 1886 at Seventh Street and Cecil B. Moore Avenue which still stands. In 1912, they built a new synagogue at North Broad and Diamond streets, which was enlarged in 1926. In 1964, their Elkins Park synagogue was completed. In 1989, the Tikvoh Chadashow Congregation of Mount Airy merged with Adath Jeshurun. In 2014, the Oxford Circle Jewish Community Center (f. 1948) Brith Israel (f. 1922) merged with Adath Jeshurun.

The Reform Congregation Keneseth Israel, the sixth oldest Reform congregation in the US, has called Elkins Park home since 1956. Formed in 1847, they built their first synagogue at Sixth and Brown streets in 1864. In 1892, their massive new synagogue was dedicated on North Broad Street. In 1951, the congregation agreed to sell the Broad Street synagogue and annex buildings to Temple University. The move to Elkins Park was completed in 1957, with many expansions and additions over the years. Many of the stained-glass windows were moved to the new Old York Road temple. The only portion of the old Broad Street synagogue that remains is the former Alumni Hall building. Temple Judea, formed in 1928 in the East Oak Lane section of North Phildelphia, merged with Keneseth Israel in 1982. Their North Broad Street synagogue was built in the 1930s with an addition in the 1950s and still stands. In 2012, Congregation Melrose Bnai Israel Emanu-El sold their Cheltenham synagogue and moved to Congregation Keneseth Israel, where they have worship and classroom space. The congregation was formed in 1957 through the merger of Bnai Israel of the Olney section of Phildelphia and the Melrose Congregation in Cheltenham. In 1985 Emanu-El Congregation (f. ca. 1925) of Philadelphia 's Oak Lane section merged with Melrose B'nai Israel.

Other congregations in Elkins Park include Kol Ami, a Reform congregation founded in 1994. In 2006 they purchased the former suburban center for Congregation Rodef Shalom in Philadelphia. The Old York Road Temple Beth Ahm was established in adjacent Willow Grove in 1947 as the Old York Road Jewish Community Center. The Reform congregation moved to Abington in 1950, and in 1959 they dedicated the Strick Auditorium. In 1975, the Molish Sanctuary was dedicated. The new Beth Torah chapel was dedicated in 2008 and is named for Temple Beth Torah, which merged with the congregation in 2004. Beth Torah, a Reform congregation, was established in Northeast Philadelphia in 1949 and chartered in 1950 as the Boulevard Temple.

Dresher is home to Temple Sinai, a Conservative congregation, which was established in the Oak Lane section of Philadelphia in 1940 and incorporated in 1941. Their first synagogue was built between 1948 and 1951 at Limekiln and Washington Avenue in Philadelphia. They built a school facility in suburban Dresher in 1971 and the present synagogue in 1978 at Limeklin Pike and Dillon Road. In the mid-1980s, Congregation Ramat-El Mount Airy Jewish Center (f. 1951) merged with Temple Sinai.

Beth David Reform Congregation in Gladwyne was established in 1943 in the Wynnefield section of Philadelphia. It was chartered in 1945 and was the fourth Reform temple in the Philadelphia area. Their original building was a large estate at 5220 Wynnefield Avenue. In 1985, they acquired a school and land from the Archdiocese of Philadelphia for their new synagogue, and in 1986 they built the present sanctuary. In 2012, the synagogue was substantially enlarged. Maple Glen is the present home of Temple Beth Or, which was established in 1954 to bring a Reform congregation to Mount Airy and other northwest Philadelphia neighborhoods. In 1955, a large mansion in Mount Airy was purchased and served as the congregation's home until 1974. That year, Beth Or purchased a mansion at Penllyn Pike and Dager Road in Spring House. A large addition was added later, and this location served Beth Or until 2006, when a new, much larger synagogue and campus were dedicated on Welsh Road in Maple Glen. The former Spring House synagogue is now a church.

A Jewish presence on Philadelphia's Main Line began in 1936 when ten Jewish businessmen formed the Main Line Jewish Association. Merion Station is home to Adath Israel, which traces its roots to the original Main Line Jewish Association. The Conservative congregation began in 1946 and purchased a home in Haverford for a synagogue. In 1949, an estate at Montgomery Avenue and Wynnewood Road in the Overbrook section of Philadelphia was purchased. By 1953, they purchased land on Old Lancaster Road and Highland Avenue in Merion Station for the first purpose-built synagogue. Abba Eban, the Israeli ambassador at the time, attended the groundbreaking for the sanctuary and school. In 1958, the final stage of construction began for the large sanctuary. Dedicated in 1959, the sanctuary, with a blue stained-glass cupola rising above, was designed by the noted architect Pietro Belluschi. An addition was built in 2003 and in that same year, Congregation Beth T'fillah merged with Adath Israel. Twenty-eight stained-glass panels from the old Beth T'fillah synagogue on Woodbine Avenue in Overbrook were installed in Adath Israel's sanctuary. Established in 1948 as the Overbrook Park Synagogue, Beth T'fillah's synagogue was built in 1951. In 1985, Temple Israel of Wynnefield (f. 1943) closed their synagogue at Woodbine Avenue and Forty-ninth Street and merged with Adath Israel. In 2010, the Suburban Jewish Community Center B'nai Aaron of Havertown closed and merged with Adath Israel.

Across the street from Adath Israel in Bala Cynwyd is the Lower Merion Synagogue. Formed in 1954 in Wynnefield, the Orthodox congregation purchased an existing structure on Old Lancaster Road, which they used until 1980, when the current synagogue was built. The facility was expanded in the 1990s. Conservative congregations, Har Zion Temple and Beth Ahm Israel, are both located on Hagy's Ford Road in nearby Penn Valley. Beth Ahm Israel was established in 1922 in Southwest Philadelphia and chartered in 1924. Their synagogue at Fifty-eighth Street and Warrington Avenue was built in 1926. The former synagogue is now a church. In 1968, the congregation built a synagogue in Penn Valley and dedicated a new, larger synagogue in 2003 on the same site. Har Zion was chartered in 1923 in Wynnefield and built their synagogue in 1924 at Fifty-fourth Street and Wynnefield Avenue. They built a large addition in the 1950s. Har Zion was the largest synagogue in the Wynnfield neighborhood. In the early 1960s, they added a campus in suburban Radnor, and in 1976 the congregation dedicated its new, consolidated home in Penn Valley. At one time, the Wynnefield section of Philadelphia had nearly two dozen Jewish congregations. Today, only Beth Tovim and RaimAhuvim, both Orthodox, remain.

Wynnewood, also on the Main Line is home to a number of large Jewish congregations, many of which have roots in Philadelphia proper. Beth Elohim-Main Line Reform Temple was established in 1952 with fifty-five founding families. By 1954, with a membership of 350 families, Main Line Reform Temple purchased the old Wynnewood mansion that had been converted into a synagogue by Temple Adath Israel. Further growth necessitated a larger synagogue, and in 1960, the current synagogue on Montgomery Avenue was consecrated. Major renovations and expansion were completed in 2005. The circular domed synagogue portion is of mid-century modern design. The dome's exterior features a Star of David. Beth Elohim was the first Reform congregation established on the Main Line. Congregation Beth Hamedrosh is located on Haverford Road in Wynnewood. The Orthodox congregation moved from their origins in West Philadelphia farther west to their new home on Brookhaven Road in the Overbrook Park section of the city in 1960. The synagogue was a modest, modern style building and is now home to a congregation of African-American Hebrew Israelites. As the Jewish population moved away from the neighborhoods adjacent to City Line Avenue, the congregation purchased land and a 1920s stone mansion in suburban Wynnewood in 2000. In 2007, they dedicated a new sanctuary on the site. In 2009, a chapel, lobby and support spaces were added to connect the old stone house with the new sanctuary. Temple Beth Hillel Beth is a Conservative congregation located on Remington Road in Wynnewood. It also has historical connections to Philadelphia proper. Congregation Beth Hillel was formed in Wynnewood in 1958. Around 1960, when the West Philadelphia Jewish Center on West Cobbs Creek Parkway and Ludlow Street closed, most of their members merged into Beth Hillel. In 1970, Temple Beth El (f. 1907) in West Philadelphia, also known as the "Rothschild Synagogue," closed and merged with Beth Hillel to become the present Temple Beth Hillel-Beth El. The current synagogue consists of the original mansion building, a sanctuary built in 1968 designed by noted architect Norman N. Rice, and a school addition built in 1990. In 2002, a structure was built to unite and expand the existing buildings.

In Montgomery County, additional synagogues include Beth Tikvah B'nai Jeshurun, a Conservative synagogue on Paper Mill Road in Erdenheim. It was created in 1973 through the merger of B'nai Jeshurun, established in Philadelphia in 1915, and Beth Tikvah of Springfield Township, established in 1956. Temple Brith Achim on South Gulph Road in King of Prussia was established in 1971 as the Brotherhood Temple Brith Achim. Their synagogue was built in 1982 and expanded in 1987 and 2008. Lafayette Hill is home to Congregation Or Ami on Ridge Pike. This Reform congregation was originally established as a Conservative congregation in 1947 in the Roxborough section of Philadelphia. It was known as the Jewish Community Group of Roxborough and in 1949 became the Ivy Ridge Jewish Community Center. The congregation relocated to Lafayette Hills in 1960 and five years later became Congregation Or Ami. The present synagogue was built in stages in 1960, 1990 and 2013. Or Hadash is a Reconstructionist congregation in Fort Washington formed in 1983. Their present synagogue, dedicated in 1995, is the former Fairwold Estate. There are Young Israel Congregations in Elkins Park (f. 1980) and Bala Cynwyd. Chabad Lubavitch has three locations in Montgomery County: their shul in Fort Washington and centers in Rydal and Lafayette Hill.

Blue Bell (Montgomery County): Congregation Tiferet Bet Israel; Exterior of the present West Skippack Pike synagogue, 1991. [Courtesy of the Author's Collection.] See also: Norristown.

Dresher (Montgomery County): Temple Sinai; Exterior of the present Limekiln Pike synagogue, 1994. [Courtesy of the Author's Collection.] See also: Philadelphia.

Elkins Park (Montgomery County): Adath Jeshurun Congregation; Exterior of the present Old York Road synagogue, 2007. [Courtesy of Arthur Rosenthal.] See also: Philadelphia.

Elkins Park (Montgomery County): Congregation Beth Sholom; Exterior of the present Old York Road synagogue, n.d. [Courtesy of the Library of Congress, Prints & Photographs Division, HABS PA,46-ELKPA,1.] See also: Philadelphia.

Elkins Park (Montgomery County: Reform Congregation Keneseth Israel; Exterior of the present Old York Road synagogue, 1994. [Courtesy of the Author's Collection.] See also: Philadelphia.

Above left: **Elkins Park (Montgomery County:** Reform Congregation Keneseth Israel; Vintage exterior of the present Old York Road synagogue, 1950s. [Courtesy of the Reform Congregation Keneseth Israel Archive.]

Above right: **Elkins Park (Montgomery County:** Reform Congregation Keneseth Israel; Vintage view of the Ark & Bima area in the main sanctuary, n.d. [Courtesy of the Reform Congregation Keneseth Israel Archive.]

Gladwyne (Montgomery County): Beth David Reform Congregation; Exterior of the present Vaughans Lane synagogue, 1993. [Courtesy of the Author's Collection.]

Maple Glen (Montgomery County): Congregation Beth Or; Exterior of the present Welsh Road synagogue, 2017. [Courtesy of Congregation Beth Or.] See also: Philadelphia and Spring House.

Maple Gen (Montgomery County): Congregation Beth Or; Sanctuary interior of the present Welsh Road synagogue, 2017. [Courtesy of Congregation Beth Or.]

Melrose Park (Montgomery County): Congregation Melrose B'nai Israel Emanu-El; Exterior of the former Cheltenham Avenue synagogue, 2008. [Courtesy of the Author's Collection.]

Merion Station (Montgomery County): Adas Israel Congregation; Exterior of the present Highland Avenue synagogue, 2010. [Courtesy of Frampton Tolbert and Mid-Century Mundane.]

Norristown (Montgomery County: Norristown Jewish Community Center-Tiferes Israel; Exterior of the former Powell Street synagogue-center, 2008. [Courtesy of the Author's Collection.]

Penn Valley (Montgomery County): Beth Am Israel Congregation; Exterior of the first Hagys Ford Road synagogue, 1992. [Courtesy of the Author's Collection.] See also: Philadelphia.

Penn Valley (Montgomery County): Beth Am Israel Congregation; Exterior of the present Hagys Ford Road synagogue, 2007. [Courtesy of Arthur Rosenthal.]

Penn Valley (Montgomery County): Har Zion Temple; Sanctuary exterior of the present Hagys Ford Road temple, 1992. [Courtesy of the Author's Collection. See also: Philadelphia.]

Pottstown (Montgomery County): Congregation Hesed Shel Emet; Exterior of the former (demolished) High and Warren Streets synagogue, n.d. [Courtesy of Congregation Hesed Shel Emet.]

Pottstown (Montgomery County): Congregation Hesed Shel Emet; Exterior of the present North Keim Street synagogue, 2017. [Courtesy of Congregation Hesed Shel Emet.]

Pottstown (Montgomery County): Congregation Hesed Shel Emet; Sanctuary interior of the present North Keim Street synagogue, 2017. [Courtesy of Congregation Hesed Shel Emet.]

Spring House (Montgomery County): Congregation Beth Or; Sanctuary exterior of the former Penllyn Pike synagogue, 1993. [Courtesy of the Author's Collection.]

Spring House (Montgomery County): Congregation Beth Or; Sanctuary interior of the former Penllyn Pike synagogue, n.d. [Courtesy of Congregation Beth Or.]

Wynnewood (Montgomery County): Beth Elohim-Main Line Reform Temple; Sanctuary exterior of the present Montgomery Avenue temple, 1993. [Courtesy of the Author's Collection.]

Wynnewood (Montgomery County): Beth Elohim-Main Line Reform Temple; Sanctuary interior of the present Montgomery Avenue temple, 2007. [Courtesy of Arthur Rosenthol.]

Wynnewood (Montgomery County): Congregation Beth Hamedrosh; Exterior of the present Haverford Road synagogue, 2007. [Courtesy of Arthur Rosenthol.] See also: Philadelphia.

Wynnewood (Montgomery County): Beth Hillel-Beth El; Exterior of the present Remington Road synagogue, 2007. [Courtesy of Arthur Rosenthol.]

City of Philadelphia

The City of Philadelphia was home to nearly 150 Jewish congregations by the 1930s, the vast majority of whom were Orthodox. At the time, Jewish neighborhoods existed in most areas of North and South Philadelphia as well West and Northeast Philadelphia. At the end of World War II, new Jewish neighborhoods were established farther west, north and northeast within the city and also in the adjacent inner-ring suburbs. Fast forward to 2018, and while the Jewish population is overwhelmingly suburban, it is still strong in city neighborhoods in Center City, Mount Airy and the Far Northeast.

The two oldest Jewish congregations established and still located in the city are Mikveh Israel Congregation and Congregation Rodeph Shalom. Mikveh Israel dates its founding to 1740, when a Jewish communal cemetery was established on Spruce Street between Eighth and Ninth streets. Many of Mikveh Israel's early members were well-known American patriots and public figures. It is the fourth oldest Jewish congregation in the US.

Mikveh Israel's first official worship space was a rented house on Sterling Alley (now Orriana Street). Their first synagogue was a two-story brick building built in 1782 at 3rd Street and Cherry Alley. A second, larger synagogue, designed by architect William Strickland, was built on the same site in 1825 and was the first building in the country to be built in the Egyptian Revival style. The third synagogue, dedicated in 1860, was located at Seventh and Arch streets. The congregation constructed its fourth building at Broad and York streets in 1909. This large Classical Revival style synagogue just north of Center City still stands. It was in use until the 1960s and looks much as it did when it was dedicated. The present synagogue was dedicated in 1976 and is less than three blocks away from the site of the congregation's first synagogue. Their current red brick synagogue is a modern and functional building. The interior contains architectural and ritual items from their previous synagogues. Of special note is the reader's platform, which is of Italian marble and dates to the 1860 building. The free-standing ark is made of oak and is silhouetted by light from the skylights above. The synagogue was home until 2010 to the National Museum of American Jewish History. The museum moved to their new building at Fifth and Market streets, and the former space is now the social hall for the congregation.

The second oldest Jewish congregation is Rodeph Shalom established in 1795, when a small group of Orthodox Jews from Germany, the Netherlands, and Poland formed a minyan for worship. Rodeph Shalom is considered the oldest Ashkenazi congregation in the Western Hemisphere. Various spaces were used for worship until 1866, when their first purpose-built synagogue was built at North Broad and Mount Vernon streets. The Moorish Revival style synagogue was designed by Frank Furness, a noted architect in Philadelphia at the time. In 1928, the architectural firm of Simon & Simon designed the present Byzantine Revival style synagogue on the same site on North Broad Street. The sanctuary seats 1,640 people, and the stained-glass windows were designed by the renowned D'Ascenzo Studio. In 2003-2004, the sanctuary was completely restored, and the building systems completely upgraded. In 1957, a suburban branch of the congregation was dedicated in Elkins Park on High School Road. That building was sold in 2007, when the congregation refocused their resources on the Center City location. The Elkins Park building now houses the Reform Kol Ami Congregation. In 2015, an extensive renovation and expansion designed by KieranTimberlake architects was completed. Rodeph Shalom is home to the Philadelphia Museum of Jewish Art.

In 1840, a third Jewish congregation, Beth Israel, was established by German and Polish Jewish immigrants. Their 1909 French and Byzantine style synagogue on North Thirty-second Street was the largest in the Strawberry Mansion neighborhood of North Philadelphia. Today Beth Zion-Beth Israel, a Conservative congregation in Center City, carries on the tradition of the original Beth Israel. It is a union of Beth Israel, Beth Zion (f. 1945) and Neziner Congregation (f. 1896), and their synagogue, a former Gothic church, is located on South Eighteenth Street in Center City. Center City also has Congregation Mekor Habracha formed in the 1990s and formalized as a synagogue in 2007 and Congregation Levy Ha-Ir, a small Reconstructionist congregation.

As Jewish immigration to Philadelphia increased in the late nineteenth and early twentieth centuries, many more congregations were formed. In the former Jewish Quarter near the Society Hill section of Center City, there are four synagogues today. B'nai Abraham is an Orthodox/Chabad congregation on Lombard Street established in 1874 as the "Russian Shul." Their Byzantine Revival synagogue was dedicated in 1910 and originally had a large onion-shaped dome. The synagogue is the oldest one in the city still used as a synagogue. Kesher Israel is a congregation also located on Lombard Street. Created in 1897 by the merger of B'nai Jacob (f. 1883) and Rodeph Tzedek (f. 1887), Beth Jacob had purchased the former Unitarian church on Lombard Street, and the merged congregation dedicated their new synagogue in 1897. In 1998, the synagogue underwent a two-million-dollar restoration. Vilna Congregation on Pine Street was formed in 1904. Their synagogue is a former row house that was completely transformed into a synagogue, complete with stained-glass windows, a round Star of David window and the name of the congregation carved in Hebrew above the entrance. It is currently a Chabad synagogue. The Society Hill Synagogue is located on Spruce Street and is housed in a former church built in 1829. In 1911, the building became the Great Romanian Shul. The building fell into disrepair in the 1960s, and in 1964 the new Society Hill Synagogue was formed. They purchased the building in 1967. The historic building has been completely restored and additions were built in 1985 and 2007.

South Philadelphia was once home to many Orthodox synagogues and prayer rooms. It had a vibrant Jewish community that rivaled that of the Lower East Side of New York City, but now is home to only a few remaining congregations. The Young People's Congregation Shari-Eli, a Conservative congregation, dates to 1952 and is housed in the former synagogue of the Orthodox Shaare Torah Congregation (f. 1928) at Franklin Street and Moyamensing Avenue. Congregation Shivtei Yeshuron Ezras Israel, "The Little Shul," has been located at 2015 South Fourth Street since 1909. The congregation was founded in 1876 and chartered in 1892. In 1961, Shivtei Yeshuron combined with Mishkan Israel and Raim Ahuvim Anshe Kalker. After decades of decline, the traditional congregation is experiencing growth and undertaking interior restoration projects. Many former synagogues in South Philadelphia still stand as a testament to the former character of the neighborhood.

North and West Philadelphia also contains dozens of former synagogues, large and small, attesting to the once vital Jewish neighborhoods. One exception in Northwest Philadelphia is the Germantown Jewish Centre established in 1936. Their first and present synagogue at Lincoln Drive and Ellet Street in the West Mount Airy neighborhood was built between 1947 and 1954. It is an impressive, modern building as seen from Lincoln Drive. The vibrant congregation today serves a diverse membership and community and is one of the foremost congregations in the city. Mishkan Shalom, a Reconstructionist congregation, formed in 1988, is also located in the Northwest section of the city in the Roxborough-Manayunk neighborhood.

The Northeast section of the city experienced growth in the number of Jewish residents and synagogues beginning in the 1920s. Many of these synagogues still stand today. After World War II, the Jewish population of the Northeast began moving further east, synagogues moved, and new congregations formed. Though the Jewish population has declined in recent years as people have moved to communities in suburban Bucks County, the Far Northeast section of Philadelphia is still home to many synagogues and Jewish community facilities with a very large Orthodox population. One of the oldest Jewish congregations in the Northeast that is still functioning is Temple Menorah Keneseth Chai formed in 1926 as the Northeast Jewish Community Center. In 1952, the current synagogue on Tysons Avenue in the Tacony section was built next to the original building. In the 1980s, Keneseth Chai merged Temple Menorah to form the present congregation. One unique congregation in the Far Northeast is Shaare Shomayim located on Verree Road. Because so many congregations that have closed in recent years have merged with Shaare Shomayim, it is now known as the Congregations of Shaare Shomayim. It was originally begun in 1962 as the Greater Northeast Jewish Congregation. The original synagogue was built in 1963, and in 1971 a larger sanctuary and addition was added to the original building. In 1989, Congregation Beth Judah joined the synagogue, and over the next two decades they also welcomed Congregation Shaare Yitzhak, Beth Tefilath Israel, Rodeph Zedek, Congregation Beth Chaim, and Congregation Beth Emeth. In early 2017, they welcomed the Ner Zedek Congregation. Ner Zedek also brought the former congregations of Adath Zion, Beth Uziel, Boulevard Park, Brith Kodesh, Ezrath Israel, and Fox Chase JCC into the synagogue community, thus preserving a large portion of Jewish history of the Northeast Jewish Community. Additional congregations in the Northeast include Beth Solomon, B'nai Israel Ohev Zedek, Temple Beth Ami and Ahavas Torah.

Above left: **Philadelphia (Philadelphia County):** Adath Jeshurun Congregation; Exterior of the former Cecil B. Moore Avenue synagogue, 2008. [Courtesy of the Author's Collection.]

Above right: **Philadelphia (Philadelphia County):** Adath Jeshurun Congregation; Exterior of the former (demolished) North Broad Street synagogue, n.d. [Courtesy of Adath Jeshurun Congregation Archives.]

Philadelphia (Philadelphia County): Beth Am Israel Congregation; Exterior of the former Warrington Avenue synagogue, circa 1930. [Courtesy of the Beth Am Israel Congregation Archives.]

Philadelphia (Philadelphia County): Beth Emeth B'nai Yitzchok Congregation; Exterior of the former Bustleton Avenue synagogue, 1990. Beth Emeth (f. 1950) and B'nai Yitzchok (f. 1924) merged in 1989. The Bustleton Avenue synagogue was built in 1959 for Beth Emeth. In 2007 the congregation closed and merged with The Congregations of Shaaray Shomayim. [Courtesy of the Author's Collection.]

Philadelphia (Philadelphia County): Beth Hamedrosh Congregation; Exterior of the now former Brookhaven Road synagogue, 1990. [Courtesy of the Author's Collection.] See also: Wynnewood, Montgomery County.

Philadelphia (Philadelphia County): Congregation Beth Israel; Exterior of the former Strawberry Mansion synagogue, 2008. [Courtesy of the Author's Collection.]

Philadelphia (Philadelphia County): Congregation Beth Or; Sanctuary interior of the former Mount Airy synagogue, n.d. [Courtesy of Congregation Beth Or.] See also: Maple Glen and Spring House.

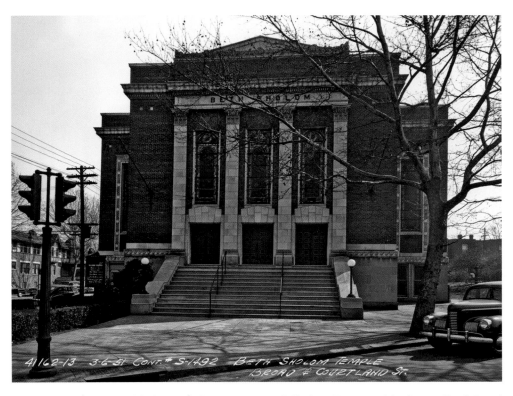

Philadelphia (Philadelphia County): Congregation Beth Sholom; Exterior of the former North Broad Street synagogue, 1951. [Courtesy of the Philadelphia Department of Records.]

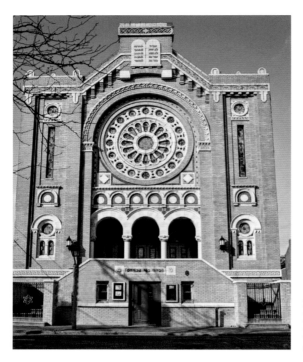

Philadelphia (Philadelphia County):
B'nai Abraham Chabad Congregation;
Exterior of the present Lombard Street
synagogue, n.d. [Courtesy of David Mink.]

Philadelphia (Philadelphia County): B'nai Abraham Chabad Congregation; Sanctuary interior of the present Lombard Street synagogue, n.d. [Courtesy of David Mink.]

Philadelphia (Philadelphia County): B'nai Jeshurun Congregation; Exterior of the former Strawberry Mansion synagogue, 2008. [Courtesy of the Author's Collection.]

Philadelphia (Philadelphia County): B'nai Yitzchok Congregation; Exterior of the former East Roosevelt Boulevard synagogue, 2008. [Courtesy of the Author's Collection.] See also: Beth Emeth B'nai Yitzchok.

Philadelphia (Philadelphia County): Congregation B'rith Israel; Exterior of the former East Roosevelt Boulevard synagogue, 1989. Established in 1922. The synagogue was built in 1930. It closed in 1990 and merged with the Oxford Circle Jewish Center which in turn closed and merged with Adath Jeshurun of Elkins Park in 2004. [Courtesy of the Author's Collection.]

Philadelphia (Philadelphia County): Congregation Beth Tefilath Israel Rodeph Zedek; Exterior of the Welsh Road synagogue, 1990. Established in 1910 Beth Tefilath Israel merged with Rodeph Zedek (f. 1953) in 1982. The synagogue, built circa 1951, closed in 1998 and merged with The Congregations of Shaaray Shomayim. [Courtesy of the Author's Collection.]

Philadelphia (Philadelphia County): Emanu-El Congregation; Exterior of the former Stenton Avenue synagogue, 2008. The congregation was formed in the 1920s and the synagogue was built between 1946 and 1951. It closed in 1985 and merged with Melrose B'nai Israel in Melrose Park. [Courtesy of the Author's Collection.] See also: Melrose Park.

Philadelphia (Philadelphia County): Germantown Jewish Centre; Sanctuary exterior of the present Lincoln Drive synagogue, 2008. [Courtesy of the Author's Collection.]

Philadelphia (Philadelphia County): Germantown Jewish Centre; Facade and entrance of the present Lincoln Drive synagogue, 1994. [Courtesy of the Author's Collection.]

Philadelphia (Philadelphia County): Har Zion Temple; Exterior of the former Wynnefield Avenue synagogue, 2008. [Courtesy of the Author's Collection.]

Philadelphia (Philadelphia County): Reform Congregation Keneseth Israel; Exterior of the Brown and Sixth Streets synagogue (demolished), n.d. [Courtesy of the Reform Congregation Keneseth Israel Archives.]

Philadelphia (Philadelphia County): Reform Congregation Keneseth Israel; Exterior of the North Broad Street synagogue (demolished), circa 1915. [Courtesy of the Reform Congregation Keneseth Israel Archives.]

Philadelphia (Philadelphia County): Reform Congregation Keneseth Israel; Sanctuary interior of the North Broad Street synagogue (demolished), 1937. [Courtesy of the Reform Congregation Keneseth Israel Archives.]

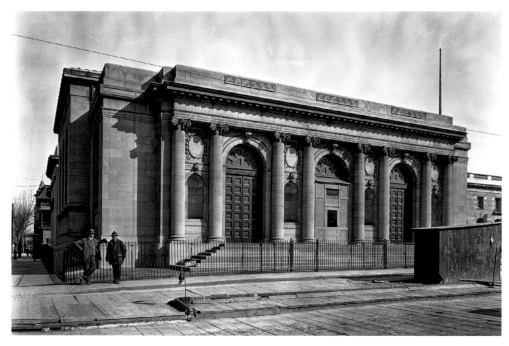

Philadelphia (Philadelphia County): Mikveh Israel Congregation; Exterior of the former North Broad Street synagogue, 1925. [Courtesy of the Philadelphia Department of Records.]

Philadelphia (Philadelphia County): Mikveh Israel Congregation; Sanctuary view towards the Ark of the present North Fourth Street synagogue, 2016. [Courtesy of Congregation Mikveh Israel and Louis Kessler.]

Philadelphia (Philadelphia County): Oxford Circle Jewish Community Center B'rith Israel; Exterior of the former Unruh Avenue synagogue, 2008. [Courtesy of the Author's Collection.] See also: B'rith Israel.

Philadelphia (Philadelphia County): Ramat El Mount Airy Jewish Community Center; Exterior of the former Johnson and Ardleigh Streets synagogue; 2008. Established in 1951, the synagogue was built in stages between 1951 and 1964. In 1984 the congregation merged with Temple Sinai in Dresher. [Courtesy of the Author's Collection.]

Philadelphia (Philadelphia County): Congregation Rodeph Shalom; Exterior of the present synagogue complex on North Broad Street; 2015. [Courtesy of Halkin Mason Photography and Congregation Rodeph Shalom.]

Philadelphia (Philadelphia County): Congregation Rodeph Shalom; Partial facade view of the present synagogue complex on North Broad Street; 2015. [Courtesy of Halkin Mason Photography and Congregation Rodeph Shalom.]

Philadelphia (Philadelphia County): Congregation Rodeph Shalom; Main Sanctuary of the present synagogue complex on North Broad Street; 2015. [Courtesy of Congregation Rodeph Shalom.]

Philadelphia (Philadelphia County): The Congregations of Shaare Shamayim; Exterior of the present Verree Road synagogue 2008. [Courtesy of Arthur Rosenthol.]

Philadelphia (Philadelphia County): Temple Beth Torah; Exterior of the former Welsh Road temple, 1992. The Reform temple closed in 2004 and merged with the Old York Road Temple Beth Am. The building is now a church and the facade has been completely remodeled. [Courtesy of the Author's Collection.]

Philadelphia (Philadelphia County): Temple Judea; Exterior of the former North Broad Street temple, 2008. Established in 1928 and built in 1939, the congregation closed in 1982 and merged with Reform Congregation Keneseth Israel in Elkins Park. [Courtesy of the Author's Collection.]

Philadelphia (Philadelphia County): Temple Menorah Keneseth Chai; Exterior of the present Tyson Avenue synagogue, 2008. [Courtesy of the Author's Collection.]

Above left: **Philadelphia (Philadelphia County):** Temple Shalom; Exterior of the former Roosevelt Boulevard synagogue, 2008. Established in 1948 and built in 1942 and rebuilt in 1992 after a fire. The synagogue closed in 2004 and merged with Beth Sholom in Elkins Park. [Courtesy of the Author's Collection.] See also: Elkins Park.

Above right: **Philadelphia (Philadelphia County):** Temple Sinai; Exterior of the former Washington Avenue and Limekiln Pike synagogue, 1990. [Courtesy of the Author's Collection.] See also: Dresher.

Philadelphia (Philadelphia County): Chabad at Vilna Congregation; Facade of the current Pine Street synagogue, 2008. [Courtesy of the Author's Collection.]

Philadelphia (Philadelphia County): West Oak Lane Jewish Community Center; Exterior of the former Thouron and Sedgewick Streets synagogue, 2008. Conservative congregation formed in 1950. Groundbreaking for the synagogue was in 1953. At the time it was one of the biggest Jewish congregations in West Oak Lane. In 1978 the congregation closed and merged with Beth Sholom in Elkins Park. [Courtesy of the Author's Collection.]

Philadelphia (Philadelphia County): West Philadelphia Jewish Community Center; Exterior of the former Ludlow Street and West Cobbs Creek Parkway synagogue (demolished), 2007. The synagogue was built in 1927/28 and closed in 1960. [Courtesy of the Author's Collection.] See also: Beth Hillel Beth El in Wynnewood.

2

The Lehigh Valley and Lebanon Valley Regions

Berks County

Berks County, which lies to the northwest of the Philadelphia region, is part of the Lebanon Valley and Pennsylvania Dutch Country. Reading, its largest municipality and county seat, was created in 1748 and settled initially by immigrants from southern and western Germany. The first documented Jewish settlers in the area were three men on a tax list from the 1750s: Lyon Nathan, Meyer Josephson, and Israel Jacobs, who made their living as traders and peddlers. A Jewish community in Reading did not develop until 1864, when the Oheb Sholom Congregation was established with sixteen charter members who also purchased a cemetery plot. Their first permanent synagogue was a former church located at Chestnut Pearl streets, which was purchased in 1884 and remodeled for use as a synagogue. The next summer, the synagogue was officially dedicated by Rabbi Isaac Meyer Wise, the leader of Reform Judaism in the United States. The building still stands today. Mount Sinai Cemetery, the first official Jewish cemetery, was founded by the congregation in 1898 on New Holland Avenue in Shillington. The old cemetery was vacated, and over time all the bodies were moved to the new cemetery.

As the congregation grew and prospered, the need arose for a larger building. In 1923, the congregation dedicated their first purpose-built synagogue at Chestnut Street and Perkiomen Avenue. This new synagogue was dedicated by Rabbi Stephen S. Wise. The Classical Revival style synagogue was in use for seventy-seven years until 2000, when a new contemporary synagogue was dedicated on Warwick Drive in suburban Wyomissing. Many items from the Perkiomen Avenue temple such as stained-glass windows, chandeliers, memorial plaques and ritual items were included in the new building. The ark and bema were built to be a replica of that which was in the Perkiomen temple. In 2014, the congregation dedicated an impressive history wall in the synagogue's rotunda. The former synagogue on Perkiomen was sold and still stands.

Beginning in 1880, the Eastern European Jewish population of Reading began to grow due to increased persecution in the Russian Empire. In 1888, Congregation Shomrei Habrith was officially chartered. In 1893 their first purpose-built synagogue at 533 North Eighth Street opened. In 1913, they built a brand-new synagogue on the same site, which still stands today. In 1962, they dedicated a new modern synagogue at 2320 Hampden Boulevard. Because the Orthodox Jewish population in Reading declined from the 1980s onward, Shomrei Habrith decided to close the synagogue in 2009. That same year, the building officially became the Chabad Center of Berks County, which had leased the building from Shomrei Habrith in 2008. In the 1960s

Shomrei Habrith had adopted the practices of Modern Orthodoxy, and a group split off in 1965 to form the Beth Jacob Traditional Orthodox Synagogue. A former church at 955 North Tenth Street was dedicated in 1966; that congregation is no longer in existence.

In 1911, a charter was granted to Congregation B'nai Zion, which purchased the old Chestnut Street synagogue, originally the first home of Oheb Sholom. A charter was granted to Congregation Kesher Israel in 1913, which then purchased a former church at Eighth and Courts streets. These two congregations merged in 1929 to form the Kesher Zion Congregation. The first purpose-built synagogue for the Conservative congregation was dedicated in 1950 at 1245 Perkiomen Avenue. As the membership of the congregation aged, the congregation faced the reality that they no longer needed such a large synagogue. The red brick classical style structure was sold in 2016. Kesher Zion currently shares space with the Oheb Sholom synagogue in Wyomissing.

One well-known Jewish family of Reading is the Boscov Family of department store fame. Solomon Boscov came to Reading from Russia in 1911 and began as a peddler. He opened his first store after World War I and began expanding in 1962. Solomon passed away in 1969, and today the family-owned department store chain operates stores in five states.

Reading (Berks County): Kesher Zion Synagogue; Exterior of the former Perkiomen Avenue synagogue, 2000. [Courtesy of the Author's Collection.]

Reading (Berks County): Kesher Zion Synagogue; Front facade the former Perkiomen Avenue synagogue, 1989. [Courtesy of the Author's Collection.]

Reading (Berks County): Reform Congregation Oheb Sholom; Exterior of the former Perkiomen Avenue temple, 1989. [Courtesy of the Author's Collection.]

Reading (Berks County): Reform Congregation Oheb Sholom; Facade of the present Warwick Drive temple, n.d. [Courtesy of Mapio.]

Reading (Berks County): Reform Congregation Oheb Sholom; Side view of the present Warwick Drive temple, 2018. [Courtesy of Reform Congregation Oheb Sholom.]

Above: **Reading (Berks County):** Reform Congregation Oheb Sholom; Sanctuary interior of the present Warwick Drive temple, 2018. [Courtesy of the Reform Congregation Oheb Sholom.]

Left: **Reading (Berks County):** Congregation Shomrei Habrith. Exterior of the former North Eighth Street synagogue, 1990. [Courtesy of the Author's Collection.]

Lebanon County

The city of Lebanon is the county seat of Lebanon County and part of the Pennsylvania Dutch region. Lebanon's first Jewish Community was formed in the eighteenth century in what is now the eastern portion of the county. Local history books tell of Jewish traders and merchants in what is now Schaefferstown (originally Heidelberg) and the surrounding area. Scant records and surviving ritual items indicate that these men were observant Jews. One of the first and most well-known of these early Jewish settlers was Barnard Jacobs, a Mohel and merchant. During the 1760s and 1770s, Jacobs had become an unofficial leader of the Jewish community in Heidelberg. He performed ritual circumcisions for the Jewish families of Heidelberg, as well as Easton, Harrisburg, Philadelphia and York. Jacobs kept a record book of his work and recorded thirty-three births in Heidelberg between 1757 and 1790. This book is the oldest surviving vital record pertaining to Pennsylvania's early Jews. The Jewish merchants of Heidelberg maintained connections to Jewish merchants and traders in Lancaster and Philadelphia; however, most of these activities came to a virtual end during the time of the Revolutionary War, and the local Jewish community went out of existence.

Jewish activity in the county did not begin again until the early twentieth century, when Jewish peddlers began to pass through the Lebanon Valley. Many of them decided to stay, put down roots and raise families. By the Jewish New Year of 1906, there were enough Jewish men in town to form a minyan for worship, and the Jewish residents of Lebanon began to plan for a congregation and house of worship. It was these early families that formalized Jewish Community life in Lebanon in 1907, when eighteen charter members established Congregation Beth Israel. After meeting in a variety of rented facilities in the city, the congregation purchased a permanent home in 1929 at 624 Chestnut Street, the vacant Emanuel Evangelical Church. They remodeled the building for use as a synagogue and added Jewish symbols to the facade of their new home. They formed a cemetery association in 1931 and purchased ground in 1933. Up until that time, Jewish burials took place in Harrisburg, Lancaster and Reading.

Space at the synagogue had become an issue by the late 1930s, but it was not until 1946 when a fundraising committee was formed to raise money for a new synagogue. 1947 saw the purchase of two lots at Oak and Eighth streets. In 1952, the noted American Jewish architect Percival Goodman was engaged to design the synagogue. The completed synagogue and center was dedicated in the fall of 1953. The old synagogue became the public library from 1953 to 1985. Goodman's synagogue is simple and modern in design, and yet imposing, with stained glass, exterior Jewish symbols and Hebrew lettering adorning the facade. Interestingly, the entrance doors to the synagogue are painted yellow, which Goodman felt would evoke the Yellow Star of the Holocaust and be an everlasting memorial to the Jews who perished. Lancaster also has a Holocaust Memorial erected by the local B'nai B'rith Lodge circa 1979. Situated on a prominent city corner, Beth Israel continues as the only Jewish congregation in Lebanon County, an active, visible Jewish religious and cultural presence in the larger community.

Above: **Lebanon (Lebanon County):** Congregation Beth Israel; Exterior of the former Chestnut Street synagogue, n.d. [Courtesy of Congregation Beth Israel and Joseph & Judith Clark.]

Below: **Lebanon (Lebanon County):** Congregation Beth Israel; Sanctuary interior and Confirmation Class at the former Chestnut Street synagogue, 1946. [Courtesy of Congregation Beth Israel and Joseph & Judith Clark.]

Lebanon (Lebanon County): Congregation Beth Israel; Exterior of the completed new South Eight Street synagogue, 1952. [Courtesy of Congregation Beth Israel and Joseph & Judith Clark.]

Lebanon (Lebanon County): Congregation Beth Israel; Sanctuary interior of the South Eight Street synagogue, 2017. [Courtesy of Congregation Beth Israel and Joseph & Judith Clark.]

Lehigh and Northampton Counties

The Lehigh Valley is home to Jewish communities in Allentown and Bethlehem in Lehigh County, and Easton in adjacent Northampton County. Jewish settlement began in the Sixth Ward neighborhood of Allentown around the time of the Civil War, but the first permanent Jewish resident was Henry Schnurmann, who had arrived much earlier, in 1847. Other German and Hungarian Jews came to Allentown over the next forty years, and the Jewish community expanded again with the arrival of Jews from Eastern Europe.

The first Jewish organization in Allentown was the Mount Sinai Cemetery Association. Two early Jewish residents and prominent merchants on Hamilton Street, Henry Schnurrman and Simon Feldman, purchased land for a Jewish burial ground in Fairview Cemetery and applied for a charter for the organization in 1875. The cemetery remained the burial place for Allentown's Reform Jews until 1928, when the Reform Congregation Keneseth Israel established their own cemetery. The first formal Jewish congregation in the city was Agudath Achim which was established sometime prior to 1887, the year the congregation obtained its first spiritual leader. Agudath Achim built their synagogue from 1892-1893 at 625 North Second Street. The Orthodox congregation was still a functioning congregation as late as 1986. Their building still stands, though its present use is not known. A second Orthodox congregation, Shaare Sholom, opened in 1916 across the street from Agudas Achim. They merged with Agudas Achim in 1950.

Congregation Keneseth Israel, though incorporated in 1903, traces its beginnings to 1883 when a group of Allentown Jewish merchants formed the Young Ladies and Young Men's Hebrew Society, today's Jewish Community Center. At the time of incorporation, the congregation began planning for their first temple. The simple yet elegant temple was built in 1906 at 31 South 13th Street in the Sixth Ward. The facade featured two small towers along with a round Star of David stained glass window. The round arched entrance also featured a stained-glass Star of David above the doors. The building, now a church, has had minimal exterior changes and still features some of the stained-glass windows and original wooden entrance doors. The congregation joined the Reform movement in 1909. By the early 1950s, the congregation had outgrown the old building. Their present temple was built in 1955 at 2227 West Chew Street. Extensive bas-relief Judaica sculptures feature prominently in the stone and marble facade. The synagogue was expanded and renovated in 1988.

Another Orthodox congregation, Sons of Israel, was established in 1903, with twenty-five members. Their original synagogue, also in the Sixth Ward, at Sixth and Tilghman streets, was dedicated in 1909. At the time, the stone synagogue was the largest and most ornate of all the synagogues in the Lehigh Valley, with imposing towers and a stained-glass rose window at the facade, plus an impressive sanctuary interior. Continued growth and the need for a larger building resulted in the new contemporary style synagogue, built in 1968 at 2715 West Tilghman Street. The red brick structure features a stained-glass tower, along with stained glass clerestory windows and exterior Judaica artwork. Congregation Sons of Israel is the only full-service Orthodox congregation in Allentown and the region.

The Conservative congregation, Temple Beth El, was formed in 1929, when nineteen founders gathered to form a congregation based on the principles of the Conservative Jewish movement, which was gaining momentum in the US at the time. Rented facilities were used until a home at 12th and Walnut streets was purchased for use as the synagogue. At the time, the congregation numbered fifty families. The need for more space was apparent when, in 1935, High Holy Day services had to be held at a rented auditorium. Despite the need for more room, the congregation waited until after the end of World War II to move forward with building their first purpose-built synagogue. In 1949, High Holy Day services were held in the new temple, though much finishing work was still in process. In 1952, they dedicated the completed synagogue at Seventeenthnd Hamilton streets. The large sanctuary featured a stained-glass dome ceiling and windows. In 1958, an educational wing was added. By 2000, the congregation had outgrown the facility and started planning for a move. In 2006, Temple Beth El's new synagogue complex was dedicated on Springhouse Road in suburban Whitehall Township. Significant parts of the old building were incorporated into the new synagogue. The stained-glass dome and windows, along with the artwork and ritual items from the old building, express the need to remember the past while still moving forward. The Hamilton Street building was sold in 2003 and demolished to make way for expansion of the adjacent hospital.

Bethlehem, also in Lehigh County, sits between Allentown and Easton and was once known countrywide as the home of Bethlehem Steel. The city's origins were as a Moravian settlement. German Jews began to settle in Bethlehem in the middle of the nineteenth century. They were primarily merchants and settled on the north side of Bethlehem. Eastern European Jews came to the city during the late nineteenth and early twentieth centuries and settled on the south side. They started out as peddlers and small shopkeepers. The first Jewish congregation to be organized was Brith Sholom, organized in 1889, and chartered the following year. A splinter group from the new congregation formed a second congregation, Talmud Torah, in 1892. Their differences were settled the following year when they reunited into one congregation now called Brith Sholom Talmud Torah. A Jewish cemetery was established around 1890 in the Fountain Hill section of the city.

In 1893 land at Wood and Walnut streets (now Summit and Carlton) was purchased on which to build the first synagogue. The cornerstone for the brick synagogue with twin domes was laid in 1897 and attended by a large crowd including non-Jewish residents. In 1925 the congregation changed the name to the Brith Sholom Community Center and a new impressive synagogue and community center at Broadhead and Packer streets was dedicated in 1926. The center was modernized and renovated in 1963 and again after a tragic fire in 1970. The need for such a large facility and the high costs associated with it came into question and in 1986 Brith Sholom relocated to their new Contemporary style synagogue at Jacksonville and Macada roads. The present synagogue was expanded in 2001. The Broadhead and Packer building still stands and is now part of Lehigh University.

The Jewish Community of Easton in adjacent Northampton County is one of the oldest in Northeast Pennsylvania. There were Jewish residents in the city before the Revolutionary War, and Myer Hart (Meyer Hart de Shira) and his wife Rachel were one of the eleven founding families of the town in 1750. Meyer was the first merchant in town, an innkeeper, and helped to fund the town's first school.

The first Jewish congregation in Easton was formed in 1839. Congregation Brith Sholom, later to become Temple Covenant of Peace, was founded by Easton Jews primarily of German origin. Until the end of the nineteenth century, sermons and records were in German. The congregation was chartered in 1842, and a temple was dedicated on South Sixth Street. It was built to resemble the Great Synagogue in Florence, Italy. Originally Orthodox in ritual, the congregation adopted the Reform ritual in 1870 after a visit by the American Reform Rabbi Isaac Meyer Wise. Covenant of Peace is the twelfth oldest Reform congregation in the US. The synagogue was in use for 117 years until 1959, when the congregation dedicated a new synagogue at Fifteenth and Northampton streets. The old synagogue was the third oldest US synagogue still standing, until it was destroyed by fire in 2003. The architect for the new synagogue was Daniel Schwartzman, known for his synagogue designs in Europe. On the grounds is one of the earliest free-standing Holocaust memorials in the country.

During the latter part of the nineteenth century, Jews from Eastern Europe came to the US, many settling in Easton. With their Orthodox origins and observance still very much a part of their daily lives, a group of these Jews formed the B'nai Abraham Congregation in 1888. By 1908, with ninety families, the congregation constructed their first synagogue, located on Ferry Street. It was a multi-story synagogue. The building, though now abandoned, still stands in Easton. The 1920s saw a push for some reforms, including the addition of a section for mixed seating and some English in the prayers. The Hebrew School was moved in 1920 to the recently opened Young Men's Hebrew Association or Jewish Community Center. The congregation hired a Conservative rabbi in 1937, but separate Orthodox services were still held until the late 1940s. The congregation made plans for a new synagogue and purchased land at 1545 Bushkill Street in 1960. In 1966, the new synagogue opened, with a sanctuary evoking the biblical Tent of Abraham. The B'nai Abraham Synagogue is within walking distance of Temple Covenant of Peace. Both congregations experienced growth after their new buildings were opened, but by the end of the twentieth century, the local Jewish population had declined. In March of 2018, B'nai Abraham Congregation and Temple Covenant of Peace announced they would merge. As of the writing of this book, the congregations plan to list both buildings for sale and will continue as a merged congregation in whichever building does not sell first. For a number of years the same rabbi, Melody Davis, has served both congregations and will continue to serve as the rabbi of the merged congregation.

Other synagogues in the greater Lehigh Valley include Temple Shirat Shalom, a Reform congregation established in 2011 in Allentown. Chabad Lubavitch of the Lehigh Valley was established in Allentown in 2001. Congregation Am Haskalah, a Reconstructionist congregation, was established around 1982 in Allentown. It met in various locations in Allentown over the years and now meets at Congregation Brith Sholom in Bethlehem. Also in Bethlehem is Congregation Beth Avraham/Anshei Sfard. This Orthodox congregation, founded in 1920, was originally incorporated as Agudath Achim in 1921. Their first synagogue was at 437 Webster Street in South Bethlehem. In 1965, they dedicated a new synagogue at 1550 Linwood Street in the borough of Edgeboro, now part of Bethlehem. Beginning in 1977, the congregation lay dormant for over two decades until 2003, when a rabbi was hired. By 2004, the congregation had grown and was renamed Beth Avraham in honor of the first rabbi of the congregation, Avraham Mowitz, who served for thirty years. Also known as Beth Avraham/Anshei Sfard, the congregation is currently planning for a new building after the 2010 sale of the Linwood Street synagogue to a Messianic congregation.

Allentown (Lehigh County): Congregation Agudas Achim; Exterior of the former North 2nd Street synagogue, 1990. [Courtesy of the Author's Collection.]

Allentown (Lehigh County): Temple Beth El; Exterior view of the present Springhouse Road synagogue, circa 2017. [Courtesy of Temple Beth El.]

Allentown (Lehigh County): Temple Beth El; Sanctuary interior of the present Springhouse Road synagogue, circa 2017. [Courtesy of Temple Beth El.]

Allentown (Lehigh County): Temple Beth El; Chapel interior of the present Springhouse Road synagogue, circa 2017. [Courtesy of Temple Beth El.]

Above left: **Allentown (Lehigh County):** Temple Beth El; Facade of Hamilton Street synagogue (demolished) with Rabbi Michael Meyerstein, 1977. [Courtesy of Temple Beth El.]

Above right: **Allentown (Lehigh County):** Congregation Keneseth Israel; Exterior of the former South 13th Street temple, n.d. [Courtesy of Congregation Keneseth Israel.]

Below: **Allentown (Lehigh County):** Congregation Keneseth Israel; Interior of the former South 13th Street temple, n.d. [Courtesy of the Author's Collection.]

Allentown (Lehigh County): Congregation Keneseth Israel; Exterior of the present Chew Street temple, 2007. [Courtesy of the Author's Collection.]

Allentown (Lehigh County): Congregation Sons of Israel; Exterior of the present Tilghman Street synagogue, 1988. [Courtesy of the Author's Collection.]

Above left: **Allentown (Lehigh County):** Congregation Sons of Israel; Exterior of the former Sixth and Tilghman Streets synagogue, 1989. [Courtesy of the Author's Collection.]

Above right: **Bethlehem (Lehigh County):** Congregation Brith Sholom; Exterior of the former Wood and Walnut Streets synagogue (demolished), n.d. [Courtesy of Congregation Brith Sholom.]

Bethlehem (Lehigh County): Congregation Brith Sholom; Exterior of the Broadhead and Packer Streets synagogue/center, circa 1926. [Courtesy of Congregation Brith sholom.]

Bethlehem (Lehigh County): Congregation Brith Sholom; Sanctuary interior of the former Broadhead and Packer Streets synagogue/center, n.d. [Courtesy of Congregation Brith Sholom.]

Bethlehem (Lehigh County): Congregation Brith Sholom; Present-day exterior of the former Broadhead and Packer Streets synagogue/center, 2018, Photograph by Micki Auerbach Wechsler. [Courtesy of Congregation Brith Sholom.]

Bethlehem (Lehigh County): Congregation Brith Sholom; Exterior of the present Macada Road synagogue, 2018, Photograph by Micki Auerbach Wechsler. [Courtesy of Congregation Brith Sholom.]

Bethlehem (Lehigh County): Congregation Brith Sholom; Interior of the present Macada Road synagogue, 2018, Photograph by Micki Auerbach Wechsler. [Courtesy of Congregation Brith Sholom.]

Easton (Northampton County): Bnai Abraham Synagogue; Exterior of the present Bushkill Street synagogue, 2017. [Courtesy of Samantha Seidel.]

Easton (Northampton County): Bnai Abraham Synagogue; Sanctuary interior of the present Bushkill Street synagogue, 2017. [Courtesy of Samantha Seidel.]

Right: **Easton (Northampton County):** Bnai Abraham Synagogue; exterior of the former Ferry Street synagogue, 1990. [Courtesy of the Author's Collection.]

Below: **Easton (Northampton County):** Temple Covenant of Peace; Exterior of present Northampton Street temple, 2017. [Courtesy of Samantha Seidel.]

Above left: **Easton (Northampton County):** Temple Covenant of Peace; Interior of present Northampton Street temple, 2017. [Courtesy of Samantha Seidel.]

Above right: **Easton (Northampton County):** Temple Covenant of Peace; Exterior of former South Sixth Street temple (demolished), 1990. [Courtesy of the Author's Collection.]

Below: **Easton (Northampton County):** Temple Covenant of Peace; Exterior sketch of the first temple, n.d. [Courtesy of Temple Covenant of Peace.]

3

The Pocono Mountain Region

P ennsylvania's Pocono Mountain Region has long been known as a vacation and honeymoon mecca. Primarily a resort area with a strong connection to Philadelphia, the close proximity to New York City also attracted guests from adjacent areas of New York State. The Pocono resorts were never defined as Jewish in the way that New York's Catskill Mountains were, but by the 1940s there were many resorts that catered to a decidedly Jewish clientele. The Jewish community in the region has never been very large, but it has a very long history. The first and oldest Jewish congregation in the region is Congregation Beth Israel located in Honesdale in Wayne County. Established in 1849, it is among the oldest Jewish congregations in Pennsylvania outside of Philadelphia.

Carbon County

Carbon County is considered to be part of Pennsylvania's vast Coal Region, and portions of the county are within the Pocono Mountain region. The borough of Lehighton is the largest municipality in the county and is home to Temple Israel. Jewish families from Lehighton and Weissboro had gathered for religious services and events in the area for two decades before Temple Israel was established in 1924 as an Orthodox congregation. The first and current synagogue on Bankway Street was built in 1924. The year after the synagogue was built, Jewish families from Palmerton also joined the congregation. As in so many small towns in Pennsylvania and across the United States, the Jewish population in Lehighton has declined from its height in the 1950s, but the congregation continues today, dedicated to being a Jewish presence in the county. Though Orthodox in the beginning, the congregation for many years has had Reconstructionist rabbis to lead services. Today the congregation is progressive and unaffiliated and is the only synagogue in the county.

Monroe County

The Borough of Stroudsburg in Monroe County has been home to Temple Israel since 1963, when their second and present building was dedicated. Their first synagogue was located in the adjacent borough of East Stroudsburg at 31 Brown Street. This first permanent synagogue for the congregation was built in 1925, just six years after the congregation was formed in 1919. This was the year that the first formal Jewish worship, for Yom Kippur, was held in town, and plans began for a congregation. Temple Israel was incorporated in 1925 as the Sons of Israel Congregation. During the 1950s the congregation joined the Conservative branch of American Judaism. By this time the synagogue building was showing signs of age and was becoming inadequate for the congregation's needs. The high cost of expanding and renovations led the congregation to consider building a new synagogue altogether. Fundraising began in 1958, and land was purchased on Wallace Street and Avenue A in Stroudsburg. The new mid-century modern style synagogue designed by John Michael was consecrated in December 1963. That same year, a residence for the rabbi and family was constructed on the temple property. The old synagogue was sold in 1966 to the Monroe County Redevelopment Authority, but no longer stands.

Stroudsburg once had many Jewish merchants, butcher shops and bakeries on Main Street. Many in the congregation refer to the period between the 1920s and 1960s as their golden age. Temple Israel remained strong as the late 1960s and early 1970s brought changes in demographics of the local Jewish community. The 1980s saw Jewish families moving to the Poconos from New Jersey and New York. Today, Temple Israel of the Poconos continues serving not only the Jewish population of the Stroudsburgs, but also the surrounding areas. In 2004, Chabad Lubavitch of the Poconos was established in Stroudsburg. It is now known as Chabad of the Mountains.

Wayne County

Honesdale, in Wayne County, is home to the historic synagogue and congregation, Beth Israel. In 1849, ten families came together to form one of the first Jewish congregations in Northeast Pennsylvania and one of the oldest in the United States. At the time of Beth Israel's founding, the borough of Honesdale was only nineteen years old. At Passover 1849, there was only one Jewish family living in Honesdale, but by the High Holy Days of that year, there were enough Jewish families to hold regular religious services. The first Jewish resident was William Weiss and his family, immigrants from Germany. At the time, all of the Jewish settlers in Honesdale were German immigrants, and the early services and records of the congregation are in German. William Weiss became one of the most prominent Jews in Honesdale.

The congregation hired its first rabbi in 1852, and by the summer of 1856 they dedicated a synagogue. The land for the synagogue on Court Street was donated by a non-Jew, R. L. Lord, Director of the Delaware and Hudson Canal Company. When money ran short to complete the synagogue, Mr. Lord came to the rescue and donated the needed funds, but with one stipulation: that a steeple be added to the building. The synagogue, which is similar in style to a New England meeting house, is still often referred to as the "Jewish Church" by locals. It is the smallest synagogue in the country that was planned and built to function solely as a synagogue. In 1962, an educational wing was added. Established as an Orthodox congregation, Beth Israel later embraced Reform. With an influx of more traditional Jews from Eastern Europe in the 1930s and 1940s, the congregation became more mainstream Reform. Honesdale has never had a large Jewish population, and there were times when the congregation did not have a rabbi. By the turn of the twentieth century, there were two congregations in town, Beth Israel and Sherith Israel. Little is known about Sherith Israel, but it is assumed that it was a splinter group that eventually merged back with Beth Israel. Beth Israel's synagogue is the sixth oldest in the United States and the second oldest to be continuously operated by the founding congregation. Only

Beth Elohim in Charleston, South Carolina is older, having been built in 1840. The Honesdale synagogue has a Star of David atop the spire and once had Gothic style stained-glass windows installed in 1933 but lost in the flood of 1942. The sanctuary interior includes a large chandelier and Tiffany globe sconces. The congregation still has members of some of the founding families, families from Northeast Pennsylvania as well as newer members who moved to Honesdale from New York, New Jersey, and Philadelphia.

Pike County

One other synagogue in the region is the Jewish Fellowship of Hemlock Farms in Lords Valley in Pike County. Hemlock Farms is a gated resort-style home community that dates to the early 1960s, located on what was once a private estate The Jewish congregation was established in 1971 as the number of Jewish families in the community grew large enough to support a formal congregation. Their synagogue, the only one in Pike County, was built in 2000.

Lehighton (Carbon County): Temple Israel; Exterior of the present Bankway Street synagogue, 2007. [Courtesy of Bernard Berlow and Temple Israel.

Above: **Lehighton (Carbon County):** Temple Israel; Sanctuary interior of the present Bankway Street synagogue, 2007. [Courtesy of Bernard Berlow and Temple Israel.]

Left: **Stroudsburg (Monroe County):** Temple Israel of the Poconos; Postcard of the present Wallace Street temple exterior and interior, circa 1960s. [Courtesy of Special Collections, College of Charleston Libraries.]

EXTERIOR
OLD TEMPLE
1925

INTERIOR
OLD TEMPLE
1925

East Stroudsburg (Monroe County): Temple Israel of the Poconos; Exterior and interior of the Brown Street temple (demolished), 1925, Dedication Journal 1965. [Courtesy of Temple Israel of the Poconos.]

Stroudsburg (Monroe County): Temple Israel of the Poconos; Exterior of the present Wallace Street synagogue, 2017. [Courtesy of Temple Israel of the Poconos.]

Stroudsburg (Monroe County): Temple Israel of the Poconos; Sanctuary exterior of the present Wallace Street synagogue, 2017. [Courtesy of Temple Israel of the Poconos.]

Honesdale (Wayne County): Congregation Beth Israel, Vintage postcard of Court Street synagogue, n.d. [Courtesy of Special Collections, College of Charleston Libraries.]

Above left: **Honesdale (Wayne County):** Congregation Beth Israel; Exterior of the present Court Street synagogue, 2017. [Courtesy of Congregation Beth Israel.]

Above right: **Honesdale (Wayne County):** Congregation Beth Israel; Sanctuary interior of the present Court Street synagogue, 2017. [Courtesy of Congregation Beth Israel.]

Honesdale (Wayne County: Congregation Beth Israel; Sanctuary and balcony of the present Court Street synagogue, 2017. [Courtesy of Congregation Beth Israel.]

4

The Anthracite Coal Mining Region

Since the middle of the nineteenth century, this region of Pennsylvania has been known for coal mining, iron and steel production, goods manufacturing, and the railroad industry. These economic engines fueled the growth of the cities and towns all across the region. Labor for these various industries came primarily from European immigrants, who came to the US seeking opportunity and stability. The formation and growth of Jewish communities throughout Lackawanna, Luzerne and Schuylkill counties was due in large part to the wealth of economic opportunities available to Jewish immigrants.

Lackawanna County

Lackawanna County, in the upper northeast portion of the state, is named after the Lackawanna River. Scranton, the county seat, is the largest city in the region and has the largest Jewish community in Northeast Pennsylvania. During the heyday of industry, mining and manufacturing, small Jewish communities existed throughout the county in addition to Scranton. Most of those synagogues have closed, and the Jewish community has been centered in Scranton for many decades. There were Jewish merchants in the city in 1810, and by 1859 there were a dozen Jewish merchants residing in the city, who had originally come from Germany. The first Jewish congregation to be established is known today as Temple Hesed. The founding families of the congregation came to Scranton in the 1840s. In 1858, an Orthodox German Jewish congregation, Chevra Rodef Sholom, was formed. In 1860, the congregation was renamed Kehilath Anshe Chesed and incorporated in 1862. Services were initially held in Scranton's Alhambra Hall. In 1867, the congregation built the city's first synagogue, on Linden Street. The synagogue was dedicated by Rabbi Isaac Meyer Wise, the founder of Reform Judaism in America. It was an elegant brick house of worship with twin towers, Romanesque architectural elements, and stained-glass windows. A large Star of David stood atop the center roof between two Italianate style towers. The synagogue was in use until 1902. when a new temple was dedicated on Madison Avenue in the Hill section of Scranton. Known as the Madison Avenue Temple of Reform Congregation Anshe Chesed, the new synagogue was a domed Moorish Revival style structure that had a stone facade with Moorish keyhole arches. Above the entrance was a large, round, stained glass Star of David window. A school and auditorium were added in 1938. In 1950, the entire facility was renovated, and the Oppenheim Chapel was added in 1957. The congregation changed their name to The Madison Avenue Temple in the 1960s. Continued growth resulted in a new temple being built in 1973 off of Lake Scranton Road. It was designed by the noted Jewish architect Percival Goodman. When the new temple was built, the congregation was renamed Temple Hesed-The Temple of Loving Kindness. It was completely refurbished in 1999.

A Conservative congregation, Temple Israel was established in 1921 by members of the Scranton Jewish Community who preferred a more traditional form of worship than that offered at the Reform temple. A former church at Monroe and Gibson streets was purchased and renovated for use as the first synagogue, and a cemetery was established in the nearby Borough of Dunmore. Interestingly, today Temple Israel manages the cemeteries of the closed Jewish congregations in Carbondale, Dickson City and Jessup. Their present synagogue was built in 1927 on the same site as their first building. It is a large domed synagogue with a facade of stone and brick. At the top of the roof cornice over the entrance is a large stone Decalogue. The main sanctuary, on the second level, seats 1,500 people and has stained glass windows and a massive stained-glass dome. The Weinberger annex and the Goodman chapel were added in 1974.

By the beginning of the twentieth century, Scranton had a large population of Orthodox Jews. They came to the city with the wave of Eastern Europeans who immigrated to the US during the late nineteenth and early twentieth centuries. The first congregation for these immigrants was Bais Hamedrash Hagadol formed in 1886 and later known as the Penn Avenue Shul and later the Penn Monroe Shul. Around 1892, the B'nai Israel and Anshe Sfard congregations were established, both having synagogues located in the Flats section of the city; the two eventually merged. Next came the Ahavas Achim Congregation in 1899. As more Jews came to Scranton, additional congregations were formed: Kneseth Israel in 1901, Ahavath Sholom in 1911, Machzikey Hadas in 1924, and Ohev Zedek in 1925. The Keneseth Israel Congregation purchased the former Linden Street Temple of the Reform Anshe Chesed and rededicated it as the Linden Street Shul in 1913. The Penn Monroe Shul was located at Olive and Monroe streets. The site is now the synagogue of the Machzikey Hadas congregation. Ahavath Sholom's synagogue was located at 1733 North Main Avenue, and the building is now a Head Start Preschool. In 1938 Ohev Zedek purchased a former church at 1423 Mulberry Street. The church was renovated for use as a synagogue and features Jewish-themed stained-glass windows and a Star of David atop the roof gable. The congregation still uses it today. The Orthodox Beth Sholom Congregation, located at the corner of Clay and Vine streets, formed around 1970 through the merger of B'nai Israel, Ahavas Achim and Beth Hamedrash Hagadol. Scranton has the largest Orthodox Jewish population in Northeast Pennsylvania and is home to schools, synagogues and kosher establishments. This particular segment of Scranton's Jewish population has grown due to the influx of Orthodox Jewish families from New York and New Jersey who commute to those cities to work.

Many of the small mining and manufacturing towns in the county also had Jewish congregations at one time. Most have closed over the years, but several of the synagogues still stand along with the local Jewish cemeteries in many of the towns. Carbondale's Congregation Agudath Shalom was established in 1907, though it may have been in existence as early as the 1890s. Their brick synagogue with stained glass windows was located on Pike Street. When the synagogue closed in the 1970s, the cornerstone was moved to the Jewish cemetery on Route 6 in Dalton. Eighty-four Jewish men from Carbondale served in both World Wars and the Korean War. One of these men was Brigadier General Alvin Ungerleider, a decorated war hero. A memorial to his legacy was recently erected in Carbondale. The growth and prosperity of the borough in the first half of the twentieth century was due in large part to the involvement of the local Jewish community.

A war memorial plaque from the congregation and a painting of the synagogue are displayed in the local historical society

Dickson City had Congregation Oheb Sholem, which was organized in 1905. Though the congregation no longer exists, their twin towered frame synagogue with small Star of David window on the facade still stands on Main Street. The Jewish cemetery in Dickson City was completely renovated in 2016 through a surprise bequest from Robert Spitz of Dickson City, who died in 2014. Dunmore's Temple Israel dates to 1908, when services began to be held in the homes of various Jewish residents. Their synagogue at 515 E. Drinker Street, built in 1925, is a white stucco building with twin towers, each capped by a Byzantine Revival style dome and Star of David. The congregation still holds Orthodox services and is the oldest Orthodox synagogue in the county to operate continuously in the same location. Jews settled in Jessup beginning around 1890 and formed the B'nai Israel Congregation. Their frame synagogue was located on Fourth Avenue. Olyphant was once home to the Bichor Cholem Congregation, which was begun around 1890. The congregation no longer exists, but their synagogue, located on Willow Avenue and Lincoln, still stands. It is a two-story building with central tower, second level sanctuary and stained glass windows. Old Forge also once had a Jewish congregation called Bichor Cholim. Their synagogue was on Church Street and later Oak Street.

Above left: **Dickson City (Lackawanna County):** Congregation Oheb Sholem; Exterior of the former Main Street synagogue, n.d. [Courtesy of the Author's Collection.]

Above right: **Dunmore (Lackawanna County):** Temple Israel; Exterior of the Drinker Street synagogue, 1990. [Courtesy of Author's Collection.]

Scranton (Lackawanna County): Congregation Beth Sholom; Exterior of the present Clay and Vine Streets synagogue, 1991. [Courtesy of the Author's Collection.]

Scranton (Lackawanna County): Congregation Machzikey Hadas; Exterior of the present Monroe Avenue and Olive Street synagogue, 1991. [Courtesy of the Author's Collection.]

Above left: **Scranton (Lackawanna County):** Congregation Ohav Zedek; Exterior of the Mulberry Street synagogue, 1991. [Courtesy of the Author's Collection.]

Above right: **Scranton (Lackawanna County):** Temple Hesed; Exterior of the former Linden Street Temple (demolished), n.d. [Courtesy of Temple Hesed.]

Below: **Scranton (Lackawanna County):** Temple Hesed; Postcard of the former Madison Avenue Temple, n.d. [Courtesy of Special Collections, College of Charleston Libraries.]

Scranton (Lackawanna County): Temple Hesed; Exterior of the present Lake Scranton Road temple, 2018. [Courtesy of Daniel Bubnis.]

Scranton (Lackawanna County): Temple Hesed; Sanctuary exterior of the present Lake Scranton temple, 1991. [Courtesy of the Author's Collection.]

Scranton (Lackawanna County): Temple Hesed; Sanctuary interior of the present Lake Scranton synagogue, 2018. [Courtesy of Daniel Bubnis.]

Scranton (Lackawanna County): Temple Israel; Exterior of the present Monroe Avenue and Gibson Street temple, 2018. [Courtesy of Daniel Bubnis.]

Above left: **Scranton (Lackawanna County):** Temple Israel; Main Sanctuary interior of the present Monroe Avenue and Gibson Street temple, 2017. [Courtesy of Temple Israel.]

Above right: **Scranton (Lackawanna County):** Temple Israel; Stained glass sanctuary dome of the present Monroe Avenue and Gibson Street temple, 2017. [Courtesy of Temple Israel.]

Below: **Scranton (Lackawanna County):** Temple Israel: Interior of the Goodman chapel of the present Monroe Avenue and Gibson Street temple, 2017. [Courtesy of Daniel Bubnis.]

Luzerne County

Luzerne County, in the Wyoming Valley, is located to the southeast of Lackawanna County. Like its neighbor county, it was an active coal mining and manufacturing center at one time. From the mid-nineteenth century to the first quarter of the twentieth, thousands of European immigrants came to Luzerne County to work in the expanding mines and related industries. Various manufacturing plants opened to take advantage of the ever-increasing labor pool. As with most Rust Belt cities, the decline in mining and manufacturing, which began by the early 1950s, took a toll on the cities and towns in the region for the next fifty years. Many synagogues in the region closed, and others faced an aging membership. Despite these facts, there are still active Jewish congregations in Luzerne County, mostly in the county seat of Wilkes-Barre, with one remaining active congregation in Luzerne Borough.

The oldest Jewish community in the county, and the Wyoming Valley, is in Wilkes-Barre. The first Jewish settlers came to Wilkes-Barre in 1838. They were Orthodox Jews, mainly originating from Bavaria and other portions of southwest Germany. They began as peddlers, shopkeepers and merchants and quickly became part of the larger community. By 1840, over a dozen Jewish families lived in the city; they held orthodox religious services and organized a Jewish cemetery and a beneficial society. In April 1845, this group organized the B'nai B'rith Congregation. The first synagogue, a two-story whitewashed brick building, was built on South Washington Street in 1849. The city's five churches donated funds to help with the building of the synagogue. Two prominent rabbis of the time, Samuel Isaacs from New York City and Isaac Leeser from Philadelphia, helped to dedicate the synagogue. The congregation was incorporated in 1885, and by 1860 it began adopting many reforms, moving away from Orthodoxy. Growth and prosperity of the congregation resulted in a new and large Moorish Revival style temple built in 1881 at 175 South Washington Street. The synagogue was used for nearly eighty years until 1959, when the present synagogue was dedicated at 408 Wyoming Avenue, across the river from Wilkes-Barre, in the neighboring Borough of Kingston. The design of the temple is simple and modern, with large, beautiful stained-glass windows. The architects of the temple included Percival Goodman, who went on to design more than fifty US synagogues. Goodman was also instrumental in the design of the Jewish Community Center building on South River Street, which began in 1863 as the Young Men's Hebrew Association.

As in many areas of Pennsylvania, Jewish immigrants from Eastern Europe came to Luzerne County seeking a better life, drawn by the opportunities of thriving industrial and manufacturing communities. They were overwhelmingly Orthodox in religious practice and began forming their own congregations. Between the late 1870s and early 1880s, Wilkes-Barre's Eastern European Jews had come together to form a worship minyan, which later resulted in the founding of several Orthodox congregations and the building of their synagogues: Anshe Emes, Anshe Sfard, Bnai Jacob and Holche Yosher. At the end of the nineteenth century, immigrants from the Austro-Hungarian Empire began settling in Northeast Pennsylvania, and a group of about twenty-five Orthodox Jewish families in Wilkes-Barre organized worship services in their homes. The group formally organized in 1892, when the Orthodox congregation was granted a charter. The new congregation was named Ohav Zedek Anshe Ungarn to reflect the fact that the members were Jews of Austro-Hungarian origin. Their first synagogue was built in 1902 on Pennsylvania Avenue (then Canal Street). The synagogue, known as the Hungarian Synagogue, was a large elegant brick building with twin towers capped by domes and a large round Star of David window above the entrance. By 1927, the growing congregation needed a larger building, so they made plans for a new synagogue at 242 South Franklin Street. In January 1932 the new and present synagogue was dedicated. As Jews of other ethnic backgrounds joined the congregation, the name was changed to Congregation Ohav Zedek of Wilkes-Barre. The synagogue's brick facade features Moorish detailing and beautiful blue and green colored tiles. The facade also features a round stained-glass window with a Star of David over the entrance. Ohav Zedek's synagogue is one of the largest in the region. As the years progressed and the need for so many Orthodox congregations decreased, the congregations of Anshe Emet, Anshe Sfard, Bnai Jacob and Holche Yosher decided to come together and form one congregation to be called the United Orthodox Synagogue. They merged in 1967, with the consolidated congregation using the synagogue built in 1922 for Anshe Emes at 13 South Welles Street. In 1999, the United Orthodox Synagogue merged with Ohav Zedek Congregation. The synagogue at 13 South Welles Street still stands.

During the 1920s, the Conservative Jewish movement began to grow in America as a bridge between Reform and Orthodox Judaism. In 1922, a group of Wilkes-Barre Jews formed Temple Israel. In 1925, their first and present synagogue was dedicated. It is a large Byzantine Revival style synagogue with a large central dome, smaller domes over the two towers that flank the entrance, and stained-glass windows over the doors, as well as a central round stained-glass window. The facade features bas-relief sculptures of Star of David and intricate brickwork. The central dome over the sanctuary features beautiful stained glass as well.

While the Jewish Community in Wilkes-Barre is stable, it is aging and has an aging infrastructure. In 2014, an ambitious fundraising plan was launched to build a Jewish Community Campus, the Friedman Center for Jewish Life, in Kingston. On the site of a former supermarket on Third Avenue, it will house a new Jewish Community Center and the offices of the Jewish Community Alliance of Northeastern Pennsylvania (formerly the Jewish Federation and Jewish Family Services). Chabad of the Wyoming Valley. which has a synagogue and center on Second Avenue in Kingston, will move its school to the new campus. Temple Israel has agreed, on a three-year trial basis, to move its offices and school to the new campus. If the need arises, the three congregations could, at some future time, sell their synagogues and build their own sanctuaries on the campus. Groundbreaking on the project began in late 2015.

Other cities and boroughs in Luzerne County once had synagogues, and several still have functioning Jewish congregations today. Some of the old synagogues still stand, but for most the Jewish cemetery is the only physical reminder of the Jewish community. Duryea was home to the Keneseth Israel Congregation from 1920 to about 1969. It was an Orthodox congregation whose synagogue was a renovated house on Newton Street. Exeter's Congregation, Anshe Ahavas Achim, was founded in 1905; their synagogue was located on Wyoming Avenue. In Freeland there existed a short-lived Orthodox congregation, Beth Sholom, which was begun in 1950. A former church was dedicated as the synagogue in 1951. The congregation closed around 1965, and the building now houses a library.

Hazleton's Jewish community was large enough to have two synagogues: Beth Israel and Agudas Israel. Though diminished in size, they still continue today. Beth Israel, a Reform congregation, was established in 1906. Their synagogue is located at 98 North Church Street. Agudas Israel was formed in 1893 as an Orthodox congregation and later transitioned to the Conservative movement. Their large classical style brick synagogue is located at 77 North Pine Street. The Jewish Community in Hazleton also once supported a modern Jewish Community Center. Dedicated in 1953 at 91 North Laurel Street, the facility closed prior to 2009 and was renovated for use as a church in 2013.

Congregation Ahavas Achim in Luzerne is the only other active Jewish Congregation in the county outside of Hazleton, Kingston and Wilkes-Barre. The Orthodox synagogue is located at 429 Walnut Street. In Nanticoke, Congregation Anshe B'nai Jehudah was established in 1915. Their synagogue was on State Street near Prospect Street and is now part of a church. Pittston once had a large Jewish congregation and synagogue. Congregation Agudath Achim began in 1907 and built a large synagogue at 62 Broad Street. In 1980, the congregation merged with Temple Israel in Wilkes-Barre. The facade of the synagogue was completely remodeled in the 1950s and 60s and now serves as a church. The Jewish cemetery located in West Pittston served the Pittston congregation, as well as those in Duryea and Exeter. Congregation B'nai Israel once existed in Plymouth Borough. Their synagogue at Church Street near Center Avenue was built from 1924-1925 and still stands. The Ahavas Jeshurun Congregation in Swoyersville was chartered about 1902, and their synagogue on the corner of Main and Kossack streets was built in1912. The congregation is no longer in existence.

Hazleton (Luzerne County): Beth Israel Temple; Exterior of the present North Church Street temple, 1991. [Courtesy of the Author's Collection.]

Above left: **Hazleton (Luzerne County):** Agudas Israel Synagogue; Exterior of the present Chestnut Street synagogue, 1991. [Courtesy of the Author's Collection.]

Above right: **Kingston (Luzerne County):** Temple B'nai B'rith; Sketch of the Washington Street Temple in Wilkes-Barre (demolished), n.d. [Courtesy of the Author's Collection.]

Kingston (Luzerne County): Temple B'nai B'rith; Exterior of the present Wyoming Avenue temple, 2018. [Courtesy of Temple B'nai B'rith. Photograph by Rabbi Roger Lerner]

Kingston (Luzerne County): Temple B'nai B'rith; Sanctuary interior of the present Wyoming Avenue temple, 2017. [Courtesy of Daniel Bubnis.]

Kingston (Luzerne County): Temple B'nai B'rith; Sanctuary windows of the present Wyoming Avenue temple, 2017. [Courtesy of Daniel Bubnis.]

Above left: **Luzerne (Luzerne County):** Congregation Ahavas Achim; Exterior of the present Walnut Street synagogue, 1995. [Courtesy of the Author's Collection.]

Above right: **Pittston (Luzerne County):** Congregation Ahavath Achim; Exterior of the former Broad Street Temple, circa 1940. [Courtesy of the Greater Pittston Historical Society.]

Below: **Wilkes-Barre (Luzerne County):** Congregation Ohav Zedek; Exterior of the current Franklin Street synagogue, circa 2017. [Courtesy of Congregation Ohav Zedek and Noam Frishman.]

Above: **Wilkes-Barre (Luzerne County):** Congregation Ohav Zedek; Sanctuary interior of the current Franklin Street synagogue, circa 2017. [Courtesy of Congregation Ohav Zedek and Noam Frishman.]

Below left: **Wilkes-Barre (Luzerne County):** Congregation Ohav Zedek; Exterior of the former Canal Street synagogue (demolished), n.d. [Courtesy of Congregation Ohav Zedek.]

Below right: **Wilkes-Barre (Luzerne County):** Temple Israel; Exterior of the present River Street synagogue, 1991. [Courtesy of the Author's Collection.]

Above: **Wilkes-Barre (Luzerne County):** Temple Israel; Sanctuary interior of the present River Street synagogue, 2018. [Courtesy of Temple Israel and Jane Messinger.]

Below: **Wilkes-Barre (Luzerne County):** Temple Israel; Sanctuary dome detail of the present River Street synagogue, 2018. [Courtesy of Temple Israel and Jane Messinger.]

Above: **Wilkes-Barre (Luzerne County):** United Hebrew Synagogue; Exterior of the former South Welles Street synagogue, 1991. [Courtesy of the Author's Collection.]

Below: **Frackville (Schuykill County):** Congregation Bnai Israel; Exterior of the former West Frack Street synagogue, n.d. [Courtesy of the Author's Collection.]

Schuylkill County

Schuylkill County, located to the south of Luzerne County, is similar in many ways to both Lackawanna and Luzerne counties with regard to the history of industry, manufacturing, and nineteenth and twentieth century immigration. Coal was prominent in the county, but it also had numerous garment manufacturers and knitting mills, many owned and run by local Jews. The oldest, and possibly the last Jewish community in the county, is in Pottsville. German Jewish immigrants came to the area and initially worked as peddlers and small merchants. The Oheb Zedek Congregation, one of the oldest in Northeast Pennsylvania, was established in 1856 with ten families. As the coal industry prospered, the number of Jewish businesses and families grew. In 1870, the congregation purchased a small frame building and had it moved to a lot on Arch Street. Rabbi Moses Phillips began serving the congregation in 1875. He peddled shirts made by his wife Endel to supplement his rabbi's income. This eventually led to the well-known company Van Heusen. The congregation built their first permanent synagogue in 1913 on West Arch Street in downtown Pottstown. With continued growth, a new synagogue-center was dedicated in 1960 at Twenty-third and Mahantongo streets. The Jewish community was so prominent at the time that the governor spoke at the dedication, which was attended by 1,000 people. By the turn of the twenty-first century, however, Pottsville's Jewish community was aging and shrinking. In 2007 they decided to sell the expansive synagogue-center on Mahantongo Street and seek smaller, more suitable quarters. In 2008, the congregation purchased a building at 2400 West End Avenue. The local Unitarian Universalist church and the synagogue share the space. Oheb Zedek established the Jewish Museum of Eastern Pennsylvania in 1987. Its collections and exhibits were housed in the 1960 synagogue and were then moved to the West End Avenue building. In 2014 the museum was closed.

Frackville's Congregation B'nai Israel (or B'nai B'rith) was located on West Frack Street and North Willow Street. The small white frame synagogue, which opened in the 1920s, is well cared for and appears to be a residence. Their yahrzeit plaque was moved to Agudas Israel in Hazleton when the Frackville congregation closed sometime prior to 2004. Mahanoy City was once home to a very active Jewish congregation, Beth Israel, formed in 1888 and incorporated in 1903. In 1923, a handsome brick synagogue was built on West Mahanoy Street, with twin domed towers, stained glass windows and Hebrew inscriptions above the entrance. Later, a small home was purchased to serve as a Jewish Community Center. Originally Orthodox, by the 1950s the congregation joined the Conservative movement. By the 1980s less than two dozen elderly Jews still called Mahanoy City home. The congregation eventually ceased to function, and the contents of the synagogue were sold, except for the many stained-glass windows that graced the synagogue. These were intended to be sold to provide an endowment fund for the care of the Jewish cemetery. They were removed in 2010 and installed in an Orthodox congregation on Long Island. The last few people connected to the Mahanoy City congregation have contended that the windows were removed without their approval. At the time of this publication. the legal claims have not yet been settled.

A small congregation called Oheb Sholem also existed in Minersville. Their synagogue opened in 1911, and a small Jewish cemetery in Mount Carbon was established in 1915. Oheb Sholem closed in 1960 when the Pottsville synagogue was opened. Shenandoah also had a substantial and active Jewish congregation at one time. Congregation Kehilat Israel was established in 1887. In 1892 a lot at 215 West Oak Street was secured and the synagogue built. The facade was remodeled and refaced during the middle of the twentieth century. There is a large, modern stained-glass window above the entrance and below it a tiled portion which spells out Kehillat Israel, along with two small menorahs. The supports of the entrance feature wrought-iron Stars of David. Kehilat Israel closed around 2005. In 2006, the historic ark from the synagogue became part of the Chabad Jewish Center of Monroe, New Jersey. At one time there was a small Jewish newspaper, *The Shenandoah Jewish Review*, and a small Jewish Community Center in town. Over one hundred members of the Jewish community served in World War II. The "Hebrew Cemetery" in Shenandoah was established in 1887 and features stone walls and entrance arches with Star of David sculptures. In nearby Tamaqua was the Sons of Jacob Congregation, begun in 1913. Their synagogue was on Schuylkill Avenue and closed around 1960. The Jewish cemetery in Hometown was also used by Mahanoy City and Shenandoah Jewish congregations.

Mahanoy City (Schuykill County): Congregation Beth Israel; Exterior of the synagogue, n.d. [Courtesy of the Mahanoy Area Historical Society.]

Right: **Pottsville (Schuykill County):** Oheb Zedeck Synagogue; Sanctuary interior and Ark view of the former West Arch Street synagogue, n.d. [Courtesy of Daniel Bubnis.]

Below: **Pottsville (Schuykill County):** Oheb Zedeck Synagogue; Sanctuary exterior of the former Mahantongo Street synagogue/center, 2008. [Courtesy of the Author's Collection.]

Above: **Pottsville (Schuykill County):** Oheb Zedeck Synagogue: Exterior side view of the former Mahantongo Street synagogue/center, 2008. [Courtesy of the Author's Collection.]

Below left: **Shenandoah (Schuykill County):** Congregation Kehilat Israel; Exterior of the former West Oak Street synagogue, 2016. [Courtesy of Ruth Ellen Gruber.]

Below right: **Shenandoah (Schuykill County):** Congregation Kehilat Israel; Sanctuary interior of the former West Oak Street synagogue, 1986. [Courtesy of Daniel Bubnis.]